D0500011

TRAILBLAZERS

33 WOMEN IN SCIENCE WHO CHANGED THE WORLD

TRAILBLAZERS

33 WOMEN
IN SCIENCE
WHO CHANGED
THE WORLD

Rachel Swaby

Delacorte Press

Library of Congress Cataloging-in-Publication Data
Names: Swaby, Rachel, author.
Title: Trailblazers : 33 women in science who changed the world / Rachel Swaby.
Description: New York : Delacorte Press, [2016] | Audience: Ages 10+
Identifiers: LCCN 2016003806 (print) | LCCN 2016004775 (ebook) |
ISBN 978-0-399-55396-7 (hardcover) | ISBN 978-0-399-55416-2 (library binding) |
ISBN 978-0-399-55417-9 (ebook)
Subjects: LCSH: Women scientists—Biography—Juvenile literature. | Women
Inventors—Biography—Juvenile literature.
Classification: LCC Q141 .S925 2016 (print) | LCC Q141 (ebook) | DDC 509.22—dc23

The text of this book is set in 11-point Garth Graphic.
Interior design by Stephanie Moss

Printed in the United States of America
10 9 8 7 6 5 4 3 2 1
First Edition

Random House Children's Books supports the First Amendment
and celebrates the right to read.

3361405783153

For Sharon, Shirley, Rosemary, and Marion

CONTENTS

HEALTH AND MEDICINE

BIOLOGY

INTRODUCTION

Most scientists and mathematicians aren't simply born brilliant. They observe and experiment and test ideas as kids and then observe and experiment and test ideas as adults. By pushing the boundaries of what they think they know, again and again, they are able to uncover something new. This process takes time, but when you're chasing after something you're really interested in—a better medication, for instance, or an unknown prehistoric creature, or a brand-new seascape deep below the surface of the ocean—the road to discovery can be positively thrilling.

This book offers a tiny glimpse at the rich history of contributions made by women to the fields of science, math, and technology. The thirty-three women included here are meant to inspire you with their extraordinary inventions and creative ideas, because you are the next generation of trailblazers who will fearlessly broaden our understanding of everything from the center of the earth to the most distant stars.

Wherever you live and whatever your age, your curiosity about the world can start right now. When Mary Anning was a child in England in the early 1800s, she found a piece of a fossilized animal in the seaside landscape around her home. She carefully dusted off the bones, making sure not to damage the specimen as she worked. Her discovery was massive. By investigating a piece of bone that sparked her interest, she found the world's first ichthyosaur skeleton.

When Sophie Kowalevski was a child in Russia, she spent her days studying the walls in her nursery. On them was a collection of her father's university work— lithographed lectures of differential and integral calculus. They were complex mathematical equations hung up after her family ran out of wallpaper. Though she did not yet understand the equations, Kowalevski later wrote, "I would stand by the wall for hours on end, reading and rereading what was written there." When she was a teenager, she plugged these equations into her lessons, accelerating through mathematics with energy and creativity. She went on to become one of the most promising mathematicians of her generation.

When the marine biologist and writer Rachel Carson was a child in the United States in the 1910s, she spent much of her time exploring her family's farm, collecting specimens and making observations: a fossilized fish, hopping birds, native plants. She started to write stories inspired by what she saw. A few of her pieces were even published in a popular children's magazine. As an adult, she wrote a book called *Silent Spring*. Its publication is credited with jump-starting the environmental movement, including the creation of the US Environmental Protection Agency.

When she was a child in Vienna, Austria, in the 1920s, Hedy Lamarr began studying the inner workings of everything from streetcars to printing presses. Lamarr eventually moved to Hollywood to be a film actress—and a most successful one, at that. Although she was glad to be acting, she started inventing things in her free time. One of her ideas would eventually usher in technologies like Wi-Fi, which delivers Internet without a cord, and the Global Positioning System, which helps pinpoint our location so that we can get places more easily.

Each woman held her curiosity tightly, as if gripping the string of a kite, and kept at her quest for answers even when it became difficult. Until fairly recently, women faced open discrimination in school and in their work. (Discrimination still happens today; but it's often harder to spot.) And yet the scientists and mathematicians here blazed their own path to discovery, understanding, and invention. Sometimes that meant setting up a secret lab, sometimes it meant examining a fragile cliff after a violent storm, and sometimes it meant looking farther, harder, and more often at the sky above us.

You can approach this book from many different angles: read it from cover to cover, dip in because there is a particular scientist you want to know more about, check out the contents page to find the topic you are most interested in, or read one entry every day. You'll likely want to share with your friends, family, teachers, or librarians some of the fascinating information you learn. For instance, kids and adults are surprised and fascinated to discover who invented windshield wipers! My goals, and yours, I hope, are to know more and to feel inspired.

TECHNOLOGY AND INVENTION

A patent provides legal protection for an original idea. In 1809, Mary Kies secured the first-ever patent awarded to a woman, for a special technique in women's hat making that weaved straw with silk.

One hundred years later, Mary Anderson puzzled over how people could drive a car in the rain and snow when the precipitation prevented them from seeing clearly out the front window. In 1903, Anderson came up with a solution, patenting the indispensable windshield wiper, upon which we still rely to keep our car windows clear today.

In basic scientific research, scientists often pursue understanding without knowing exactly where it will take them. They're interested in something like how our bodies store and use energy, so they work to gain knowledge of those systems. That process is beautifully described by biochemist Gerty Cori, the first woman to win the Nobel Prize in physiology or medicine: "As a research worker, the unforgotten moments of his life are those rare ones, which come after years of plodding work, when the veil over nature's secret seems suddenly to lift and when what was dark and chaotic appears in a clear and beautiful light and pattern."

It is in this way that Cori discovered and gave her name to the Cori cycle, which explains our body's metabolism. Inventors, however, often approach their work in reverse, identifying a problem and then working toward developing a solution. In 1981, the ophthalmologist Patricia Bath pioneered a new laser surgery to correct cataracts—cloudy deposits that can make seeing difficult. Using lasers instead of inserting instruments in the eye, Bath developed a way to make the procedure less painful for patients.

The problem Bath wanted to solve was directly related to her work as an ophthalmologist. But for others, like the movie star Hedy Lamarr, a problem out in the world can inspire a surprising solution completely unrelated to a day job. Lamarr was deeply bothered by how infrequently US torpedoes hit their targets during World War II. She thought of a solution while playing the piano and refined her idea in her living room, using items such as matchsticks that she had around the house. Her idea paved the way for Wi-Fi and Bluetooth.

In other words, inspiration is everywhere. A better solution is the one we create.

As the ecologist Rachel Carson wrote, "The materials of science are the materials of life itself. Science is part of the reality of living; it is the what and the how and the why of everything in our experience." And it is ours for the exploring.

ADA LOVELACE

1815–1852
Mathematics · British

Ada Lovelace (born Augusta Ada Byron) was given a famous name before she made her own. Her father was Lord
Byron, the bad boy of English Romantic poetry, whose
epic mood swings could be topped only by his string of
scandals. Only one month after the girl was born, little
Ada's mother had had enough of her father. She took the
baby and quit the marriage. Lord Byron left England and
never returned.

However brief their time in each other's company, Lord
Byron was ever present in Ada's upbringing—as a model
of what not to be. Worried that she might lean toward the
lyrical, Ada's math-loving mother pushed a practical curriculum of grammar, arithmetic, and spelling on the child.
When Ada became sick with the measles, she was bed-
ridden, and permitted to rise to a sitting position for only
thirty minutes a day. Any impulsive behavior was system-
atically tamped down.

It may have been a strict upbringing, but Lovelace's

mother did provide her with a solid education—one that would pay off when she was introduced to the mathematician Charles Babbage. The meeting occurred in the middle of her "season" in London, that time when noblewomen of a certain age are paraded around to attract potential suitors. Babbage was forty-one when he made Lovelace's acquaintance in 1833. They hit it off. And then he extended the same offer to her that he had to so many: come by to see my Difference Engine.

Babbage's Difference Engine was a two-ton, hand-cranked calculator with four thousand separate parts, designed to expedite time-consuming mathematical tasks. Lovelace was immediately drawn to the machine and its creator. She would find a way to work with Babbage. She *would.*

Her first attempt was in the context of education. Lovelace wanted tutoring in math, and in 1839, she asked Babbage to take her on as his student. The two corresponded, but Babbage didn't bite. He was too busy with his own projects. He was, after all, dreaming up machines capable of streamlining industry, automating manual processes, and freeing up workers tied to mindless tasks.

Lovelace's mother may have tried to purge the girl of her father's influence, but as Lovelace reached adulthood, her Byron side started to emerge. She experienced stretches of depression and then fits of elation. She would fly between frenzied hours of harp practice and the concentrated study of biquadratic equations. Over time, she shook off the behavioral constraints imposed by her mother and gave herself over to whatever pleased her. All the while, she produced a steady stream of letters. A playfulness emerged. She signed her letters to Babbage "Your Fairy."

Meanwhile, Babbage began spreading the word of another project: his Analytical Engine, a programmable beast of a machine rigged with thousands of stacked and rotating cogwheels. It was just theoretical, but the plans were to far exceed the capabilities of any existing calculators, including Babbage's own Difference Engine. In a series of lectures delivered to an audience of prominent philosophers and scientists in Turin, Italy, Babbage unveiled his visionary idea. He had convinced an Italian engineer in attendance to document the talks. In 1842, the resulting article came out in a Swiss journal published in French.

A decade after their first meeting, Lovelace remained a believer in Babbage's ideas. With this Swiss publication, she saw her opening to offer support. Babbage's Analytical Engine deserved a massive audience, and Lovelace knew she could get it in front of more eyes by translating the article into English.

Lovelace's next step was her most significant. She took the base text from the article—some eight thousand words—and annotated it, gracefully comparing the Analytical Engine to its antecedents and explaining its place in the future. If other machines could calculate, reflecting the intelligence of their owners, the Analytical Engine would amplify its owners' knowledge. It would be able to store data, and programs that could process it. She also saw the possibility for the machine to process more than numbers, suggesting that "the engine might compose elaborate and scientific pieces of music of any degree of complexity or extent."

Reining in easily excitable imaginations, Lovelace also explained the engine's limitations ("It can follow analysis; but it has no power of anticipating any analytical relations or truths") and illustrated its strengths ("the Analytical Engine weaves algebraic patterns just as the Jacquard-loom weaves flowers and leaves").

The most extraordinary of Lovelace's annotations was her so-called Note G. In it, she explained how a punch-card-based algorithm could return a scrolling sequence of special numbers, called Bernoulli numbers. Her explanation of how to tell the machine to return Bernoulli numbers is considered the world's first computer program. What began as a simple translation, as one Babbage scholar points out, became "the most important paper in the history of digital computing before modern times."

Babbage corresponded with Lovelace throughout the annotation process. She sent Babbage her commentary for feedback, and where she needed help and clarification, he offered it. Scholars differ on the degree of influence they believe Babbage had on Lovelace's notes. Some think that his mind was behind her words. Others, like journalist Suw Charman-Anderson, call her "[not] the first woman [computer programmer]. The first person."

For what it's worth, Babbage himself was effusive about Lovelace's contributions. "All this was impossible for you to know by intuition and the more I read your notes the more surprised I am at them and regret not having earlier explored so rich a vein of the noblest metal."

Lovelace possessed a strong confidence in the range of her own abilities. In one letter, she confided, "That brain of mine is something more than merely mortal. . . . Before ten years are out, the Devil's in it if I haven't sucked out some of the lifeblood from the mysteries of the universe, in a way that no purely mortal lips or brains could do."

Today, we celebrate her contributions to computer science. The US Department of Defense named the computer language Ada after her. Ada Lovelace Day celebrates the extraordinary achievements of women in science, technology, engineering, and math. The Ada Lovelace Edit-a-Thon is an annual event aimed at beefing up online entries for women in science whose accomplishments are unsung or misattributed. When her name is mentioned today, it's more than a tip of the hat: it's a call to arms for women to take up science and math.

HERTHA AYRTON

1854–1923
Physics · British

When early theatergoers nicknamed cinema "the flicks," the name was an affectionate reference to a technological quirk. The powerful light beam directed through film strips fluttered, sending black-and-white moving images to the screen in bursts and dips. That flicker came from early projectors' arc lighting, which was created when two carbon rods placed next to each other were electrified. The electricity jumped the gap between the two rods, causing a brilliant, if unsteady, arc. Over time, arc lighting's flicker was verbally shortened to *flick*, and the name stuck despite modern cinema's steady projections.

Arc lighting dates back to 1807, but it wasn't until generators caught up with the technology's needs in the 1870s that the industry could finally use it. Too bright for homes, arc lights became the go-to solution for lighthouses and other applications where very strong beams were needed. By the 1890s, they started to replace gas in streetlights.

They later became famous for their place in films. Arc lights both illuminated the sets of movies like *Citizen Kane* and beamed early silent-film stars onto the screen.

Arc lighting should have been background, but because the lights hissed and sputtered, they claimed a prominent part in every production. The ruckus occurred in the light's rods. When they were electrified, carbon evaporated and a tiny hole formed. As air rushed into the divot, it created a whine. As a result, arc-light attendants were always busy, constantly tweaking and adjusting the rods in an effort to coax them into doing their job without too much of a hiss.

Scientists like Hertha Ayrton, a British inventor and physicist, and her husband, William, an electrical engineer, started working toward a quieter and more consistent arc light in the late 1800s. Unfortunately, their work went up in flames when it was mistaken for kindling, crumpled by the maid, and tossed into the fireplace. (No word on whether the fire burned brighter.) Ayrton's husband was away in the United States on business, so Ayrton restarted the research by herself.

She began by mounting a thorough investigation. By understanding the process's intricacies, she hoped to identify the problem and figure out how to engineer the light in a way that would cut the hiss and flicker.

When she discovered that the rod was the problem, Ayrton designed one shaped for quieter use. Along the way, Ayrton also learned about the light's flutter and how the relationship between the voltage drop across the arc, the arc's length, and the current affected it. In 1895 and

1896, she published twelve papers in the *Electrician* that explained her findings.

Ayrton demonstrated her work on arcs for the Royal Society in 1899. A newspaper gushed that the "lady visitors" were "astonished . . . one of their own sex [was] in charge of the most dangerous-looking of all the exhibits—a fierce arc light enclosed in glass. Mrs. Ayrton was not a bit afraid of it."

Members of the Royal Society, however, were a bit afraid of her. When Ayrton's paper "The Mechanism of the Electric Arc" was accepted in 1901, the society recruited a male member to publicly present it, because women weren't allowed. A year later, she earned a nomination to join the society, but the group consulted a lawyer who decided that her gender made her ineligible. According to English common law, a married woman had no legal standing separate from her husband's.

Ayrton thought that the discrimination she faced was utter nonsense. "Personally I do not agree with sex being brought into science at all," she explained to a journalist. "The idea of 'women and science' is entirely irrelevant. Either a woman is a good scientist or she is not; in any case she should be given opportunities, and her work should be studied from the scientific, not the sex, point of view."

Ayrton was one of the good scientists. Her 450-page book, *The Electric Arc,* became the standard on arc lighting nearly as soon as it was published in 1902. But it wasn't until two years later that the Royal Society allowed Ayrton to read a paper of her own. Finally, the organization gave Aryton some recognition. In 1906, Ayrton was awarded the society's Hughes Medal "for an original discovery in the physical sciences, particularly as applied to the generation, storage and use of energy." Membership, however, was still out of her reach.

Until 1918, women weren't allowed to vote in England. Informed by her own early poverty and continuing experience with sexism, Ayrton was an outspoken advocate for women's voting rights, operating with authority, charm, and presence. She cared for suffragist hunger strikers and refused to participate in the 1911 census. Across the official census form she wrote, "How can I answer all these questions if I have not the intelligence to choose between two candidates for parliament? I will not supply these particulars until I have my rights as a citizen. Votes for women. Hertha Ayrton."

Ayrton was one of a small club of women attempting to gain acceptance in overwhelmingly male scientific institutions. Ayrton counted Marie Curie among her closest friends and often stuck up for the chemist's reputation publicly. "An error that ascribes to a man what was actually the work of a woman has more lives than a cat," wrote Ayrton in response to claims that Curie's husband, Pierre, was really the brains behind their scientific discoveries. When Pierre died in 1906 and Ayrton's husband, William, died in 1908, both women went on to prove that though their husbands were valued collaborators, they were highly skilled scientists on their own.

Science was actually Ayrton's second career. Before her exploration into arc lighting, she was an inventor, patenting a device that would divide a line into equal segments.

(Some biographers ascribe her affinity for tinkering to her watchmaker father.) During World War I, dismayed by reports of chlorine gas being used on British soldiers, she was drawn to invention again. The self-assigned task was this: how could she protect soldiers from the noxious gas? To experiment with a variety of methods, Ayrton staged a miniature war zone in her drawing room, with matchboxes serving as trenches, and cooled smoke (produced from brown paper lit on fire) standing in as gas. Ayrton poured the smoke over the circuit to see how it would behave. There she refined what she believed to be the best solution—essentially a big fan. It looked like a long broomstick topped by a large rectangular paddle, designed to force the gas away when flapped manually.

The military was initially skeptical. The organization's hang-ups partly had to do with the invention's name. "Fans" were objects that women carried. How could they protect men at war? It took a couple of years and a demonstration in the field in 1917, but the military finally put the devices to use; some one hundred thousand were eventually shipped to the western front. Two years later, Ayrton completed an automatic version to force away gas carried on more powerful winds.

Ayrton was a creative problem solver. She had the flexibility and skills to tackle a hiss, a flicker, or a deadly gas, whether it required a set of pillboxes or the principles of physics.

HEDY LAMARR

1914–2000
Technology · Austrian

When Hedy Lamarr (born Hedwig Kiesler) was a child, she wandered the streets of Vienna with her father, listening to him explain the inner workings of complicated machines like streetcars and printing presses. He put a high value on independence: "[My father] made me understand that I must make my own decisions, mold my own character, think my own thoughts." He provided her with marching orders to find her own way in the world. When Lamarr made the decision to leave school at sixteen and move to Berlin to pursue acting, she knew her father would not stop her.

Lamarr quickly made a name for herself on the stage and screen. But her ascent was not without snags. She married a wealthy (and persistent) munitions dealer named Friedrich "Fritz" Mandl, who promptly forced her to quit her public career as an actress. He wanted her at home. Becoming an accessory used to thrill her husband's powerful friends, however, did not suit her. "Any girl can be glamorous," Lamarr said. "All you have to do is stand still and look stupid."

Before long, Lamarr began plotting her escape. "I've never been satisfied," said Lamarr. "I've no sooner done one thing than I am seething inside to do another thing." While she performed her act as a well-coiffed houseplant, she paid careful attention to the sensitive conversations her husband was having with his guests, who included diplomats, politicians, generals, and the fascist Italian prime minister Benito Mussolini. Lamarr planned to leverage any intelligence she'd gathered against her controlling husband, should he refuse to allow her to quit the marriage. It never came to that. By 1937, after Mandl stormed off to one of his hunting lodges following a fight, Lamarr left for London with two large trunks, two small ones, three suitcases, and as much jewelry as she could carry. (Money was difficult to take out of the country.) Upon arriving, she was able to arrange an introduction to the head of MGM Studios, Louis B. Mayer, the executive with the largest salary in the United States. They met at a small party. Unlit cigar in hand, he offered her a $125-a-week contract with MGM if she could find her own way to California. Lamarr turned him down. Lamarr knew her value—and it was more than he was offering.

But Lamarr also understood that Mayer was her best ticket to Hollywood, so when the MGM head and his wife hopped on a 1,028-foot ocean liner to the United States, Lamarr made sure she secured herself a spot on the ship, too. By the time the boat arrived stateside, Mayer had upped his offer: five hundred dollars a week for seven years if she agreed to English lessons and a name change. Her new moniker, decided over a Ping-Pong table while they traveled across the Atlantic Ocean, was marquee-ready. At age twenty-two, Hedwig Kiesler walked off the ship newly anointed as Hedy Lamarr. She was cast in her first Hollywood film seven months later.

As her career ramped up, Lamarr realized she wasn't especially fond of Hollywood in the off hours—too many social occasions with "people who kid all the time," she said. Lamarr preferred time to herself to tinker. Restless and still engaged in how the world worked, Lamarr transformed her drawing room into a workshop where she could fiddle with the many ideas that preoccupied her. There, she reimagined everything from facial tissue disposal to soda. Lamarr convinced the high-flying manufacturing magnate Howard Hughes to loan her two chemists to help transform a bouillon cube into a savory cola. In *Forbes* magazine years later, Lamarr laughed about the effort: "It was a flop."

By 1940, the headlines about World War II became bleaker. Two British ocean liners carrying children to safer waters were torpedoed by German U-boats back-to-back. In the second incident, seventy-seven children were killed by people who spoke Lamarr's mother tongue. She was both shaken and incensed. She deeply wanted to find a way to help the Allied forces. Perhaps, she thought, all that information she'd gathered on German military ammunition might be of use in defending against the Germans.

Lamarr was so serious about getting the information

to officials in the United States that, for a time, she considered quitting acting in order to lend her knowledge of Mandl's dealings to the National Inventors Council, a group established during World War II as a clearinghouse for ideas submitted by the public that might help the war effort. Instead, she decided to design something practical, a technology that the military desperately needed: a better way to guide torpedoes.

By 1942, US torpedoes had a whopping 60 percent fail rate. The weapons, which were improperly tested before deployment, were fired like bowling balls with spin but no aim. They would often dive too deep, burst too early, or do nothing at all. On other occasions, the torpedoes hit enemy ships, but without enough oomph to sink them. The weapons needed better guidance to keep them on course. Lamarr started thinking about communication. If the soldiers ordering the torpedoes could keep tabs on them en route, the effect would be like installing bumper lanes in the vast, uncertain sea. Should the missile start to veer off, a human could remotely correct its path.

Engineers had been thinking about the communication problem for decades, but they hadn't yet uncovered a solution that was enemy-proof. Although radio could offer a connection between sub and torpedo, the technology had an oversharing problem. Once a station was established, enemies could easily gum it up, jam it, or listen to the signal. The line was too public. What soldiers needed was a way to talk to their weapons without the enemy overhearing the instructions. A US Navy engineer suggested an anti-jamming technique in 1898, but his solution—transmitting over higher and higher frequencies—wouldn't have lasted long as opposing forces one-upped each other for higher and higher real estate. (Frequency describes the number of radio waves that occur in a certain amount of time. So higher frequencies have densely packed waves like tight stitches on a shirtsleeve. Lower frequencies have loosely spaced waves like ripples on a pond.)

Lamarr, however, had another idea about how to secure a safe and clear connection. Since riding on a single frequency left the communication vulnerable, she thought that a coordinated effort where both the sender and the receiver hopped frequencies in a pattern would confound anyone trying to listen in. The idea was similar to two pianos playing in unison. Instead of playing the same key over and over, the two pianos would play the same song, jumping from note to note, making it harder for someone who didn't know the song (in this case, the Germans) to catch on.

Helping her to advance the idea was Lamarr's friend George Antheil, a composer who wrote movie scores to help support his more experimental musical work. Antheil was famous for a piece of music he produced in Paris in 1926 titled *Ballet Mécanique.* Although humans ended up playing the parts, the work called for automated player pianos to perform in sync. Lamarr, also an accomplished pianist, sometimes played piano with Antheil recreationally. The duo liked to chase each other across the keys. It worked like this: One person would start playing a tune, and the other would have to catch the song and play alongside. According to Lamarr's son, this synchronized musical discourse gave the inventor her idea for outsmarting the Axis opponents. By this point, Antheil had already put quite a lot of thought into how to synchronize machines. He was also once employed as a US munitions inspector. Theirs was an ideal partnership. Over countless hours on the phone, in the evenings, and spread out with matchsticks and other knickknacks on Lamarr's living room rug, the pair nailed down the basics for their frequency-hopping invention. They applied for a patent in June 1941.

More concerned about the war than monetization, Lamarr and Antheil also sent their ambitious plans to Washington, DC, for review by the National Inventors Council. The positive feedback was swift. In a special to the *New York Times,* the council leaked the idea's approval. The article began, "Hedy Lamarr, screen actress, was revealed today in a new role, that of an inventor. So vital is her discovery to national defense that government officials will not allow publication of its details." The idea was classified "red hot" by the council's engineer.

The bombing of Pearl Harbor changed the navy's perception of the project. With the tragedy came many revelations about the sorry state of the United States' existing torpedoes. At this point, the navy decided that they had neither the bandwidth nor the interest to test another system. Lamarr and Antheil secured the patent but lost out on a government contract. Lamarr's patent was classified and filed away, its inventors' chances for real-world deployment left in the dusty back pockets of a government cabinet.

It wasn't until two decades later that the idea resur-

faced, wrapped into a new frequency-hopping communication technology (later called spread spectrum). Even
then, the idea didn't go public until 1976—thirty-five years
after Lamarr patented it.

As it turned out, the technology had broader uses than
missiles alone. Lamarr's idea paved the way for a myriad
of technologies, including wireless cash registers, bar code
readers, and home control systems, to name a few. While
she had a long career as a celebrated actress, Lamarr finally got the full recognition she deserved when she was
awarded the Electronic Frontier Foundation's Pioneer
Award in 1997. Her response: "It's about time."

RUTH BENERITO
1916–2013
Chemistry · American

The cotton industry was in a tailspin. In 1960, it produced a cushy 66 percent of the clothes in American homes. By 1971, cotton's market share was cut nearly in half. Nylon, polyester, and other lab-made synthetic materials developed in the 1930s and 1940s had charmed their way onto hangers. Sure, synthetics had drawbacks. They held on to body odor and could get itchy. But they also performed this one really outstanding trick: synthetic fabrics didn't require an iron.

Cotton's wrinkling problem is a product of the material's weak hydrogen bonds. At the molecular level, the fabric is made up of strong chains of cellulose connected by hydrogen. Washing the cotton causes the cellulose chains to flap around. Meanwhile, the hydrogen atoms sit idly by, doing nothing to restore the order. Even after being pulled from the line or from the dryer, cotton clothing has wrinkles. To smooth the cellulose, you need an iron.

Morning after morning, Americans held up two shirts: one that required setting up a cloth-covered table, a hot metal object, and some spare time, and another that could be yanked from a clean laundry pile and buttoned up immediately. Synthetic fabrics didn't require as much work. They were unstoppable.

Or at least, it looked that way until 1969, when Ruth Benerito saved the cotton industry from collapsing. Her discovery of wrinkle-free cotton brought the material back from the brink.

It's important to note that Benerito had a habit of downplaying her abilities. On going into chemistry: "I'm not good with my hands. My mother said she didn't know why I went into chemistry 'cause I was so terrible with my hands." On discovering wrinkle-free cotton: "Any number of people worked on it."

Graceful motor skills or not, Benerito jumped into the women's college at Tulane University when she was fifteen. By the time she was nineteen in 1935, she'd earned her bachelor's degree in chemistry. The year was a lousy one for an aspiring chemist looking for employment. The Great Depression made it impossible for her to land a job in her field, so she took a position teaching high school and waited it out. The window of opportunity finally opened during World War II, when spots vacated by men in industry and in universities were opened up to women. Benerito taught at Tulane, finally getting her PhD after the war.

Looking back on her life and education, Benerito realized she had benefited from two separate incredible moments in scientific research. The first occurred while she attended PhD classes at the University of Chicago in the summer. "It was a good education because I was taught . . . by the greatest chemists of the last century," she mentioned nonchalantly. She was there when the university served as a Manhattan Project hub. Several of her professors were Nobel Prize winners, and some classes were so small that Benerito was in the company of just one or two other students. "I think that's what gave me such a good background in chemistry," she said. The Cold War—"when [the government] put a lot of money into science because we were competing with Sputnik"—was also favorable for Benerito and her colleagues.

Between the two periods, she returned to Tulane to teach at the engineering school. She enjoyed watching students succeed, but eventually the promotions given to her less experienced male colleagues grated on her. When a new dean came in, she asked for a raise. He replied that he'd need some time to personally evaluate her performance. It was a blatantly obvious brush-off if she'd ever seen one. "I said I've been here thirteen years. If you don't know me now, you'll never know me," she said. "So I quit."

Some former students who'd gotten jobs at the US Department of Agriculture saw Benerito's resignation as their opportunity to rope a major talent. She was hired in 1953 for what would become a very productive thirty-three-year career. The purpose of the USDA's New Orleans outpost was to push America's farm products into the future with data, science, and engineering. Benerito came to the post full of ideas and initiative.

This time, her abilities didn't go unnoticed. Within five

years, Benerito was named leader of the lab that would make fabric history. Remember those breakable bonds between long cellulose chains? To strengthen those connections, Benerito experimented with shorter bonds that would "cross-link" the longer fibers, acting like a series of rungs on a ladder. When washed and dried, the cross-links would hold the long cellulose chains in place, convincing them to lie flat for wrinkle-free fibers.

She wasn't the first one to try cross-linking. But previous attempts caused cotton fibers to act strangely. Some became so rigid that just sitting down could produce a Hulk-like effect, splitting the treated shirt all the way up the back.

Benerito's big innovation was in the additive. Instead of going with an additive that chemically attached to the cellulose chains, she found one that smoothed the surface. Her innovation not only kicked off the "wash and wear" cotton industry, but also provided the foundation for stain-resistant and flame-retardant fabrics. Benerito earned the Lemelson-MIT Lifetime Achievement Award and the USDA's highest honor for service—twice!

Though she would feel uncomfortable claiming the title, the Queen of Cotton had been crowned.

STEPHANIE KWOLEK

1923–2014
Chemistry · American

In a paper published in 1959, titled "The Nylon Rope Trick," Stephanie Kwolek and a coauthor explain how, with the right ingredients, anyone can produce the chemistry equivalent of "pulling a string of silk handkerchiefs out of a top hat." To magically pull nylon from a beaker, first you layer diacid chloride and a solvent on top of an equal amount of diluted aliphatic diamine, which sit together like oil and water. But dip a wand into the intersection of the two fluids and pull up—and voilà! A net of nylon appears like a circus tent, gathering at the top to form a string. So much of the stuff can be lifted from the solution that one modern experimenter attached the thread to an automatic drill, powered it on, and let the nylon coil continuously around the bit.

The reaction was an impressive piece of chemical showmanship, but Kwolek's next trick would be death-defying. In 1964, she designed a fabric that could stop a speeding bullet.

If someone had asked Kwolek as a child what she believed she'd be doing as an adult, she would not have said this. When she was young, Kwolek loved fabrics and sewing, so she imagined that one day she might be a fashion designer. Kwolek's mother talked her out of it, fearing that Kwolek's tendency toward perfection would lead her to starve should she find herself unsatisfied with a hem. After cultivating a love for science, Kwolek changed her mind, hoping for a career in medicine.

In 1946, she graduated with a degree in chemistry from Carnegie Mellon University in Pittsburgh. Without any luck getting loans, Kwolek had to put medical school aside until she could afford it. Thankfully, DuPont hired Kwolek as a chemist right out of college. After going in for an interview, she asked her would-be boss to speed up his decision, as she had another opportunity pending. He prepared the offer letter then and there. She later mused that it was likely her assertive style that got her the position.

The idea was that Kwolek would put in a few years at DuPont in order to save the money she needed to become a doctor. But a funny thing happened on the way to medical school. Kwolek may not have been designing clothes, but she was using chemicals to create new, futuristic fabrics. The threads she set out to create would challenge the concept of what a material is capable of—a feat that would change the course of history. When Kwolek compared her opportunities at DuPont to what she'd get out of medical school, her earlier aspirations faded. Kwolek's adventures in chemistry were just too rewarding to give up.

Furthermore, DuPont was in the middle of a particularly vibrant period. The company was experimenting with all sorts of ways to make synthetic materials mimic the incredible properties of nature. Spider silk's strength and elasticity, for instance, had been the inspiration for the invention of nylon in the 1930s. Even thirty years later, the company continued to strive for better synthetics. In the 1960s, DuPont asked Kwolek to design a replacement for steel reinforcement in tires. They needed a material that was both lighter and stronger than the metal.

In this task, Kwolek attempted to make a liquid polymer by combining two crystallized ones. Typically, when polymer A was mixed with polymer B, it created a clear, thick goop that could be spun into string. But when Kwolek repeated the process at lower temperatures, the result was a liquid—neither goopy nor clear. Repeating the experiment under the same conditions, Kwolek got an identical result. Her colleagues were dubious. The foggy mixture looked like a candidate for the trash, not one for production. The technician responsible for spinning liquid polymers into string initially hemmed and hawed, fearing that the liquid might gunk up his machine. But Kwolek stood by her work and pushed to take it further. The result was a thread of incredible lightness and strength never before seen in a lab. In 1964, Kwolek invented Kevlar.

"It wasn't exactly a 'eureka moment,' " Kwolek admitted to a local paper. Even though the fiber's readings were off the charts—five times as strong as steel and most certainly lighter—she wanted to be absolutely sure that she had her data in order, because once she revealed her results to the company, she had a pretty good feeling that DuPont would immediately spend time and money on the project.

Even after showing her results, Kwolek admitted, "I never in a thousand years expected that little liquid crystal to develop into what it did." With the attention of an entire team at DuPont, Kevlar's properties became even more remarkable.

Because of its strength and exceptionally light weight, Kevlar has been applied to everything from oven gloves to space suits to cell phones. In bulletproof vests, Kevlar has protected more than three thousand one hundred law enforcement officers from bullets.

Kwolek's preparation of the cold-spun threads launched a brand-new area of research around liquid crystalline polymers. For her work on Kevlar and her subsequent contributions to Lycra and spandex, Kwolek won the Lemelson-MIT Lifetime Achievement Award in 1999.

Whipping that strange, cloudy liquid into super-strong strings proved to be an extraordinary trick.

GRACE MURRAY HOPPER

1906–1992
Computer Science · American

When Grace Hopper was a child, she was powerfully drawn to gadgets. At age seven, she wanted to know how an alarm clock roused her family out of bed each morning. So Hopper took the thing apart. When she couldn't put it back together again, she dismantled another one. Still stumped, she tried another. When she'd pulled the screws and springs from seven machines, Hopper's mother made a deal with the child: she could tinker with one. (Later in life, Hopper coined the saying, "It's always easier to ask forgiveness than it is to get permission." She started experimenting with that one early.)

Supported by a mathematics-loving mother and an encouraging father, Hopper began her education at Vassar College at age seventeen, earning a degree in mathematics in 1928. From there she went to Yale University, knocking out both a master's and a PhD in mathematics (the first woman at Yale to do so) before returning to Vassar to teach math, the subject she loved.

For Hopper, everything changed when Japan bombed Pearl Harbor in 1941. Hopper, at age thirty-four, wanted to do something tangible for her country; she wanted to enlist. Sure, she was sixteen pounds underweight and, by average enlistment standards, very old. Sure, the government thought her vocation as a math professor was too important to leave. But Hopper was confident and determined. She wangled a leave of absence from Vassar, arranged a waiver for her weight, and in December 1943 succeeded in joining the US Navy Reserve.

In the reserve, Hopper was assigned a post in the navy's Bureau of Ships Computation Project at Harvard University. Her reputation as an excellent mathematician preceded her. As she arrived, her supervisor greeted her by asking, "Where have you been?" He immediately put her to work on the organization's massive Mark I computer, charging her with learning "how to program the beast and to get a program running."

For a mathematician with a gadget obsession, the Mark I—at fifty-one feet long and weighing five tons—was a dream with a staggering processing rate: some seventy-two words and three operations calculated every second. Hopper was its lead programmer.

The 561-page manual she wrote for the machine was groundbreaking, according to a computer historian. "The instruction sequences . . . are thus among the earliest examples anywhere of digital computer programs."

She's also known for another discovery. Every time we call a computer glitch a bug, we should give a little nod to the "Grand Lady of Software." Because if it weren't for Hopper and the moth she found wedged in the hulking

Mark II computer's relay, the computer bug might have been known by any other name.

Hopper played such a significant part in the early history of computing that her influence, like technology itself, appears everywhere. Her résumé would say she was a computer programmer—and she was—as important to the development of computers as Charles Babbage and Ada Lovelace.

After she was released from active duty, Hopper chose not to return to Vassar. She had ornery computers to wrestle, and she was having too much fun.

In 1949, Hopper moved to the Eckert-Mauchly Computer Corporation in Philadelphia, where she helped design the first electronic digital computer for large-scale commercial use. She also returned to what she'd identified as a problem with programming: It was very specialized and very dull. At the time, programmers had to manually enter every 1 and 0. Long strings of 1s and 0s were how programmers talked to their computers. But it was boring! What humans needed was a translator, a program that would take reasonable human commands and transform them into the binary language—the 1s and 0s—of computers. Never the type to wait to have things done for her, Hopper designed one. Her program, A-0, which stands for "automatic programming language zero," is now known as the first "compiler." In the history of programming languages, adding the ability both to interact with the machine more intuitively and to pack more into a command was hugely significant. Instead of having to input strings of 1s and 0s to explain to the computer what it needed to do, Hopper packed those strings into, say, one letter on a keyboard.

She also provided the foundation for COBOL (common business oriented language), a programming language designed specifically for business use. Even today, COBOL remains a major player in business and government organizations.

In 1966, Hopper retired from the Navy Reserve. It didn't last long. Her presence was requested for a six-month stint to work on automatic data processing, at which point the navy made it clear that her services would be required indefinitely. Hopper was promoted to captain and then, in 1977, became the special adviser to the commander of the Naval Data Automation Command. During her second stint in the navy—one that lasted nineteen years post-"retirement"—she helped set common standards for the organization's programming languages. Those standards made their way to the Department of Defense and then into all of our computers.

Long before Apple popularized the slogan Think Different and *disruptive* became a Silicon Valley mantra, Hopper lectured students, colleagues, and technology companies against using what she called "the most damaging phrase in the language." The statement that stopped good ideas was, said Hopper, *"We've always done it this way."* Hopper was so adamant about banning the saying that she, dressed in her full navy uniform, often threatened to—poof!—"come back and haunt" the poor souls who dared to utter it. In any case, the idea has remained a core tenet of technology. Today, the worst thing you can say about a new idea is that it's safe. As a constant reminder to rethink even those things we consider fundamental, Hopper's office clock ticked counterclockwise.

As she got older, Hopper would stroll confidently down a conference hall corridor with a group trailing behind her, and people would routinely turn in awe. At the podium, she was a captivating visionary, exciting listeners with predictions about the future of computers. She often challenged the audience to think more creatively.

Once, when she was asked about the boundaries of a certain technology, she replied, "They'll only be limited if our imaginations are limited. It's all up to us. Remember, there were people who said the airplane couldn't fly."

THE EARTH AND STARS

As young girls in the Northeast United States, Maria Mitchell and Annie Jump Cannon both looked up at night and were transfixed by what they saw: a vast black sky filled with glittering stars announcing their presence in the universe. With telescopes and new techniques, the two women observed structures in space as no human before them had.

In 1932, Amelia Earhart's solo flight across the Atlantic proved that women could fly planes. As an eight-year-old, Yvonne Brill heard about Earhart's extraordinary journey and decided that she was capable of similar heights. In the 1940s, Brill was likely the only woman in the United States working in rocket science. She spent her career contributing to machines that traveled into space: satellite propulsion systems, space shuttle engines, and the *Mars Observer.*

But for some women, it was not enough to send up machines and men. In 1983—twenty-two years after the

first man went into space—Sally Ride became the first
American woman to pierce Earth's atmospheric boundary.
As a NASA astronaut, her two trips into space inspired
generations of women to follow in her footsteps. Former
US Air Force colonel and retired space shuttle commander
Eileen Collins was one of them. Before Ride, there were no
American women who were astronauts. Since Ride, forty-
eight other women (as of 2015) have rocketed skyward.

Each scientist and mathematician in this chapter followed their dreams past what other people expected of
them. In 1847, Maria Mitchell shocked the world when
she became not only the first American to spot a comet,
but also the first woman to do so. The Russian mathematician Sophie Kowalevski, who lived in Germany, repeatedly
won over those skeptical about her academic abilities by
showing that she was more than capable of keeping up—
she was, in fact, a standout student and mathematician.

Once these scientists became established, they often
gave back. Both Yvonne Brill and Sally Ride spent the latter
part of their careers supporting other women interested in
the sciences. Brill lobbied for women engineers, working
to get them the recognition they deserved. And Sally Ride
founded Sally Ride Science, which encourages kids to get
into science, technology, engineering, and mathematics,
with a special focus on girls and people of color. Both Brill
and Ride hoped to connect the next generation of scientists
to the stuff of dreams: space and the stars and our ability
to touch them, either with science or in a space suit.

MARIA GAETANA AGNESI

1718–1799
Mathematics · Italian

Maria Gaetana Agnesi was a child prodigy. When visiting scholars dropped by her home in Milan, Italy, Agnesi's father trotted her out to entertain them. She was expected to recite long speeches from memory in Latin or to participate in discussions about philosophy or science with men who made these disciplines their life's work. Brought up on Cicero's letters, Virgil's poetry, and books like *How to Learn Latin Quickly,* Agnesi was the oldest of twenty-one children and was often called upon to help her father climb the social ranks. Her younger sister, a brilliant harpsichordist and composer, was also tapped to impress visitors with her extraordinary abilities.

When Agnesi was twenty-one, she realized that her participation in these showcases was not, strictly speaking, compulsory. She broke the news to her father that she had other plans for her future. Agnesi wanted to enter a convent. The announcement came on the heels of a grand display of Agnesi's scholarly ambition. In a nearly two-hundred-point document, Agnesi listed the theses she would be capable of publicly defending, in addition to all the ones she already had. However, Agnesi was shy and tired of flashing her intellect for her father's social gain. She wanted to give herself over to God.

Agnesi's father wasn't thrilled with the idea. She possessed an extraordinary brain, and he preferred that she use it. The father and daughter struck a deal. If she agreed to continue her mathematics research, Agnesi could do as much charity work as she pleased from home. He agreed that the public performances could also stop.

A late-blooming mathematician, Agnesi began seriously studying the subject only in her late teens. As with so many other academic pursuits, she took to it immediately. She studied amid globes and mathematical instruments, plowing through calculus before anyone else in Milan was studying it.

Perhaps Agnesi began her next project as a way to pass her knowledge on to her younger siblings. Or maybe she realized how annoying it was to have mathematics instruction spread out into individual branches and one-off books so that getting an education required hunting down a whole collection of resources and hiring a tutor to fill in the gaps. Whatever the case, Agnesi saw a need for a unified textbook covering algebra, geometry, and calculus. So she wrote one.

When Agnesi decided to take on a project, she went big. In 1748, she published a two-volume, 1,020-page text called *Instituzioni Analitiche,* believed to be the first mathematics book published by a woman. Agnesi had a printing press brought into her father's home so she could oversee the book's typesetting and verify that her formulas were accurately represented. If a particularly unwieldy equation ran past the bottom of the page, it was printed on a long sheet of paper that was folded up and tucked into the regular-size pages.

Agnesi wrote the book in Tuscan, the dialect that would become modern Italian, instead of her own Milanese. Because she chose Italian over Latin—the language of scholars and one she knew well—it appears the text was aimed at a school-age population from the very beginning. *Instituzioni Analitiche* would provide generations of Italian students with a solid and well-rounded mathematics education.

In England, John Colson, a professor at Cambridge University, heard about the book and the impact it was making abroad, and felt that British students urgently needed access to the same information. Getting on in age, Colson scrambled to improve his Italian so that he could translate Agnesi's text. But he hadn't yet published the translated manuscript when he died in 1760. The work was finally released in 1801 in English, thanks to a vicar who edited and shepherded it through the publication process.

More than 250 years later, Agnesi's name continues to appear in calculus textbooks: she lends it to a curve that rolls over a sphere like a gentle hill. She wasn't the first to discover the curve, although many thought she was at the time; mathematics historians found someone who had claimed the curve earlier. The "witch of Agnesi," as this curve is called, is actually the product of a mistranslation. In *Instituzioni Analitiche,* Agnesi calls her cubic curve *versiera,* which meant "turning in every direction." John Colson translated it as *versicra,* or "witch."

When her text was published, Agnesi received many accolades, including a diamond ring and jewel-encrusted box from Empress Maria Theresa, to whom the book was dedicated. Pope Benedict XIV, who was a regular correspondent of Agnesi's, recommended her for a professorship at the University of Bologna. She declined.

In 1752, when Agnesi was thirty-four, her father died and she was finally able to claim her freedom. She gave up mathematics and her other scholarly pursuits in order to spend the rest of her life serving the poor. She donated her entire inheritance to the cause. Agnesi passed away in 1799 in one of the poorhouses she had directed.

Because of her mathematical contributions and the decades she'd spent providing for others, her hometown once lobbied for her sainthood. Her greatest legacy, however, is the witch.

MARIA MITCHELL

1818–1889

Astronomy · American

Maria Mitchell worked as a librarian by day, but it was her other office—a makeshift observatory on the roof of her parents' home in Nantucket, Massachusetts—that was her favorite workspace. She worked there amid spiders and bugs and a stray cat, on both frigid nights and warm ones, studying the stars. "One gets attached (if the term may be used) to certain midnight apparitions," Mitchell wrote in her diary in 1854.

Mitchell started "sweeping the heavens" with her telescope as a child. Her father, who was an astronomer and teacher, was fond of dragging his ten kids upstairs in the evening to stargaze. For her siblings, it was a familial obligation. For Mitchell, it would become her life's work. On October 1, 1847, as she'd done many times before, Mitchell snuck upstairs while her family entertained guests—and this time she caught an extraordinary show. With a puny two-inch telescope, she spotted a smudge not visible

with the naked eye (an indication of her skill as an astronomer). When she ran down to tell her father she'd caught a
comet in her sight, he wanted to announce it immediately.
But Mitchell was cautious. Before taking credit for anything, she wanted to observe the streak more closely to
make absolutely sure she had it.

At age twenty-nine, Mitchell became one of the first
Americans to discover a comet and chart its orbit. Her
achievement made international headlines, and Mitchell became an instant scientific celebrity. The comet was
named Miss Mitchell's Comet. In her honor, she was
awarded a gold medal for the achievement by the king
of Denmark, and she was voted into the American Academy of Arts and Sciences. "Fellow"—the customary title
for male members—was erased and "Honorary Member"
replaced it.

"For a few days Science reigns supreme—we are feted
and complimented to the top of our bent . . . one does enjoy
acting the part of greatness for a while!" Mitchell wrote.
But she also reserved an eye roll for what she came to
view as an unnatural welcome. "It is really amusing to find
one's self lionized in a city where one has visited quietly
for years; to see the doors of fashionable mansions open
wide to receive you, which never opened before. I suspect
that the whole corps of science laughs in its sleeves at the
farce."

The next wave of attention came in the form of job offers. She did observational work for the US Coast Survey,
which by 1849 paid Mitchell a salary of three hundred
dollars. In 1865, Mitchell accepted a position at Vassar Col-

lege, which came with access to a top-of-the-line twelve-inch telescope. Giving her students hands-on time with the tools of the trade, however, was significantly trickier. The all-female student body had a curfew, so astronomy classes were to be held in broad daylight. Astronomy without the night sky? Mitchell was a high-profile hire without patience for ridiculous regulations.

She swiftly loosened the school's grip on her students. Mitchell lobbied for them to be able to participate in more immersive activities, including stints as the government's official eclipse observers in locations across the country. After Mitchell talked her way into a lecture at Harvard, bulldozing past a reluctant professor ("I asked him if I might attend. He said, 'Yes,' but he didn't look happy!"), she sent "her girls" at Vassar off to sit in on the Harvard professor's lectures, too. Mitchell's students adored her for advocating on their behalf and for her egalitarian teaching style. "It meant so much to come into daily contact with such a woman!" one pupil wrote. "There is no need of speaking of her ability; the world knows what she was. . . . Perhaps one clue to her influence may be found in her remark to the senior class in astronomy: 'We are women studying together.' "

During her lifelong dedication to the sky, Mitchell observed the moons of Saturn and Jupiter, sunspots, and nebulae; and she was instrumental in inspiring another generation of women to look to the sky and do the same. After her death, she was immortalized in the starry landscape she so adored: a crater on the moon was named in her honor.

EMMY NOETHER
1882–1935
Mathematics · German

Albert Einstein was in over his head. He had worked out his general theory of relativity, but he was having problems with the supporting mathematics. So Einstein pulled in a team of experts from the University of Göttingen to help him formulate the concepts. The team was led by David Hilbert and Felix Klein. The pair was admired for their contributions to mathematical invariants. But their legacy, in part, was their ability to spot talent. For the Einstein project, Emmy Noether was their draft pick.

Noether had been steadily making a name for herself in mathematics. Noether's specialty was invariants, or the unchangeable elements present during transformations like rotation or reflection. For the general theory of relativity, her knowledge base was crucial. Einstein needed interlinked equations, and Noether helped him create them. Her formulas were elegant, and her thought process and imagination enlightening. Einstein thought highly of her work, writing, "Frl. Noether is continually advising me in my projects and . . . it is really through her that I have become competent in the subject."

Noether's closest colleagues quickly realized that she was a mathematical force, someone of extraordinary value who should be kept around on a permanent basis. However, Noether faced sharp opposition. Many of the people who supported the push to make her a lecturer at Göttingen also believed that she was a special case. In general, they believed women shouldn't be allowed to teach in universities. In the end, the government wouldn't allow it. The Prussian ministry of religion and education, whose approval the university needed, shut down her appointment to the university: "She won't be allowed to become a lecturer at Göttingen, Frankfurt, or anywhere else."

The shifting political landscape finally gave Noether an opening into academia. When Germany was defeated in World War I, socialists took over and gave women the right to vote. There was still a movement at the university to get Noether on staff, and Einstein offered to advocate for her. "On receiving the new work from Fräulein Noether, I again find it a great injustice that she cannot lecture officially," he wrote. Finally, Noether was allowed a real position at the university, but her title sounded like fiction. As the "unofficial, extraordinary professor," Emmy Noether would receive no pay. (Her colleagues joked about the title, saying "an extraordinary professor knows nothing ordinary, and an ordinary professor knows nothing extraordinary.") When she finally did receive a salary, she was Göttingen's lowest-paid faculty member.

Pay or no pay, at Göttingen she thrived. Noether was a founder of abstract algebra. And according to a physicist quoted in the *New York Times:* "You can make a strong case that her theorem is the backbone on which all of modern physics is built."

She was deeply engrossed in her work. As she solved a problem in front of the class, she'd fill up the blackboard and clear it and fill it up and clear it again in rapid succession. When she got stuck on a new idea, students recalled her hurling the chalk to the floor and stomping on it, particles rising around her like dust at a demolition.

Noether would get so excited discussing math that neither a dropped piece of food at lunch nor a tress of hair sprung from her bun would slow her down for a second. She spoke loudly and exuberantly and, like Einstein, was interested in appearance only as it related to comfort. Einstein loved his gray cotton sweatshirts when wool ones were the fashion. Noether wore long, loose dresses, and cut her hair short before it was in style. For Einstein, we call these the traits of an absentminded genius. For Noether, there was a double standard—her weight and appearance became the subject of persistent teasing and chatter behind her back. However, like the annoyances of title, pay, and politics, the comments didn't bother Noether. When students tried to replace hairpins that had come loose and to straighten her blouse during a break in a particularly passionate lecture, she shooed them away. Hairstyles and clothes preferences would evolve, but Noether's dedication to math was unchangeable.

Noether was social, and generous with sharing ideas. Many important papers were sparked by her brainpower and published with her blessing but without her byline.

Though Noether had established herself as one of the greatest mathematical minds of the twentieth century, the Nazis judged her only by her left political leanings and her Jewish ancestry. In May 1933, Noether was one of the first Jewish professors fired from Göttingen. Even in the face of blatant discrimination, perhaps naively, the math came first. When she could no longer teach at the university, Noether tutored students illegally from her modest apartment. She even taught math to Nazis who showed up at her place in full military gear. It wasn't that she agreed with what was happening, but she brushed it aside, preferring to focus on her students. "Her heart knew no malice," remembered a friend and colleague. "She did not believe in evil—indeed it never entered her mind that it could play a role among men."

For her generosity, Noether's friends were wholly dedicated to her. Understanding that staying in Germany would put her in serious danger, in 1933, Noether's friends arranged for her to take a position at Bryn Mawr College in the United States. It was meant to be a temporary post until she could land somewhere more prestigious. But just two years after she arrived, Noether died while recovering from surgery on an ovarian cyst. She was fifty-three. Following her death, Einstein wrote a letter to the *New York Times*. It read, "Fräulein Noether was the most significant creative mathematical genius thus far produced since the higher education of women began." Today, some scientists believe her contributions, long hidden beneath the bylines and titles of others, outshine even the accomplishments of Einstein himself.

SOPHIE KOWALEVSKI

1850–1891
Mathematics · Russian

Sophie Kowalevski believed it was a mistake of the uninformed to confuse mathematics with arithmetic. Arithmetic was just a pile of "dry and arid" numbers to be multiplied and divided. Mathematics was a world of elegant possibilities that "demand[ed] the utmost imagination." To engage in mathematics fully was to elevate it to an art not unlike poetry. "The poet must see more deeply than other people, and the mathematician must do the same."

Looking deeply into the numbers was a skill Kowalevski acquired at a very young age. When she was a child, her father, who had recently retired from Russian military service, moved the family to a rural estate near the Lithuanian border. It was a large home next to a forest and on a lake, far from any big cities. They ordered wallpaper from St. Petersburg to freshen up the home's interior, but when the paper arrived, it became clear that there had been a miscalculation. The nursery was left bare. Instead of going through the hassle of ordering more wallpaper, Kowalev-ski's father fashioned an inexpensive, DIY solution. He had the room papered with the lithographed lectures on differential and integral calculus from a course he'd taken as a young officer. Often there is one event that excites the imagination, sending us, for the rest of our lives, restlessly after our passions; for Kowalevski, this was it. Her govern-ess could not tear the girl away from the equation-layered room. "I would stand by the wall for hours on end, reading and rereading what was written there." She was too young to understand their meaning, but that didn't stop her from trying.

For the majority of her childhood, Kowalevski's educa-tion could not keep pace with her curiosity. Her father wasn't keen on the idea of "learned women." Consc quently, her formal instruction was spotty. "I was in a chronic state of book hunger," she wrote in her autobiog-raphy. Kowalevski would sneak into her family's library to consume the forbidden foreign novels and Russian pe-riodicals heaped on the room's tables and couches. "And here, suddenly at my fingertips—such treasure! How could anyone not be tempted."

When her uncles visited, she probed them for stories about math and science. "The meaning of these concepts I naturally could not yet grasp, but they acted on my imagi-nation, instilling in me a reverence for mathematics as an exalted and mysterious science which opens up to its ini-tiates a new world of wonders, inaccessible to ordinary mortals."

Kowalevski whipped through a borrowed algebra book,

ducking the attention of her governess while she studied. When a neighbor, a physics professor, dropped off a textbook he'd written, as a gift for her father, the volume mysteriously ended up in his daughter's possession. The next time the professor visited the house, Kowalevski engaged him in conversation about the math in his book. The professor was reluctant to talk to her about something she couldn't possibly understand. She was young—at this point in her teens—and female. But Kowalevski's ability to creatively solve problems changed his mind.

The professor appealed to her father, comparing Kowalevski and her considerable abilities with the famous French mathematician Pascal. He argued that she needed advanced academic training right away.

Her father finally gave in. Kowalevski's opportunities in Russia, however, had a well-established ceiling. Her only chances for greater academic and professional development were abroad. But how to get there? Unmarried, she was stuck at home, subject to her father's rules. Married, she would be forced to conform to her husband's life in Russia. To Kowalevski and her older sister, Anyuta, neither option was viable. Kowalevski took a third option, a more unconventional one. She entered into a marriage not for love but for education.

Her husband, Vladimir Kowalevski, was part of a radical political group fighting for equal education for women. When Sophie married Vladimir at age eighteen, both she and her sister were free to leave Russia.

Kowalevski's first stop was Heidelberg, Germany. (Her husband went elsewhere to study geology.) But when she arrived, Kowalevski found that women were barred from university enrollment. The young mathematician, however, was practiced at using her insight as a tool to change reluctant minds. Kowalevski soon gained approval to attend lectures unofficially. One classmate, Yulya Lermontova, who became the first Russian woman to earn a doctorate in chemistry, remembered the impression Kowalevski made on the place. "Sofya immediately attracted the attention of her teachers with her uncommon mathematical ability. Professors were ecstatic over their gifted student and spoke about her as an extraordinary phenomenon. Talk of the amazing Russian woman spread through the little town, so that people would often stop in the street to stare at her."

Next, Kowalevski traveled to Berlin, where she convinced a mathematician she greatly admired, named Karl Weierstrass, to teach her privately. (The University of Berlin, where Weierstrass taught, had an even stricter ban on women.) He was no supporter of women entering university, but Kowalevski's abilities and passion for the subject quickly earned her a place as his star student and later a trusted peer.

She wanted a doctorate in mathematics, so Weierstrass worked out a way for her to earn one from the University of Göttingen—a university that would grant higher degrees to women—without Kowalevski having to attend class or exams. From Berlin, Kowalevski became the first woman in Europe to earn a PhD in mathematics. Most doctoral students opted to write one dissertation; Kowalevski assembled three: two in pure mathematics and one in astronomy.

Kowalevski published several groundbreaking papers,

and in 1883, Stockholm University invited her to become a lecturer. She initially rejected the invitation, citing "deep doubts" about her ability to excel at the position until she felt ready to live up to the honor. However, within six months of her arrival, she'd been promoted to full professor and offered an editor position at the journal *Acta Mathematica*. Two years later, she was the department chair, fluent in Swedish, and dedicated to her work with a singular passion not felt since the early days of liberation from her father.

It was then, egged on by supportive peers, that Kowalevski went after what the discipline called the "mathematical mermaid," a classical mathematical problem that had eluded many greats. For advancing the field's understanding of this problem, the Paris Academy of Sciences would issue a cash prize. Kowalevski worked furiously to complete her submission on time.

The Paris Academy of Sciences' announcement was a shock for two reasons. First, the winner broke so much new ground on the problem that the prize's governing body voted to increase the monetary reward. The second was a surprise only to those who didn't already know her. Of the fifteen entries submitted anonymously, Kowalevski's took the prize. Her solution led the way to new areas of research in theoretical mathematics. One analysis of her work pointed out that her win had an even broader influence: "The value . . . is not only in the results themselves nor in the originality of her method, but also in the increased interest she aroused in the problem . . . on the part of researchers in many countries, in particular Russia."

By the time of her death from pneumonia at age forty-one, Kowalevski had risen to the top of her discipline. As was custom, her brain was weighed and assessed, the size and grooves judged as an indication of ability. "[The] brain of the deceased was developed in the highest degree," reported the Stockholm newspapers. "And was rich in convolutions, as might have been predicted, judging by her high intelligence."

ANNIE JUMP CANNON

1863–1941

Astronomy · American

The human eye should be able to see about eight thousand stars dappling the night sky, location and weather conditions permitting. Now observe this: over the course of her career, astronomer Annie Jump Cannon classified fifty times that many—a record that lasted long after her death.

With a number like 400,000, Cannon started young. She established her first observatory in her parents' attic. With no trees obstructing the view, Cannon could stargaze through a trapdoor in the roof. Success for the evening was a three-pronged endeavor: First, she had to check the visibility; next, she had to light a candle made of animal fat; finally, she had to flop open a hand-me-down constellation book. Then and only then was she able to truly immerse herself in Delaware's evening sky.

Although her mother, an amateur astronomer, set Cannon upon the skyward path, her father worried over the evening tradition: "Father was more interested in the safety of the house than in the movements of the stars and it was a sigh of relief which he breathed when the evening vigil was over with the house unburned." It wasn't until his daughter attended Wellesley College that her make-shift setup would cause a problem. On another roof but under the same sky, Cannon failed to notice that a lamp she'd placed in a friend's window had started "smoking like a small engine." By the time she got to it, the room had reached the point of near-total char. Cannon called off her observations and spent the remainder of the evening scrubbing down the furniture. The walls ultimately had to be repapered.

Pyrotechnic issues aside, Cannon's time at Wellesley only reaffirmed her devotion to the cosmos. In 1896, after earning her master's degree, Cannon started as a research assistant at Harvard College Observatory. Her goal: to capture light from distant stars in order to decode the secrets it contained.

When Cannon declared stellar spectra as her specialty near the turn of the century, the method of learning about stars by examining their light was a discipline on the rise. It ran parallel to another up-and-coming area of research, which looked at what happens to stars over time, how they changed from birth to middle age to extinction. Because a single star's life cycle takes place over too great a period for humans to observe, astronomers began gathering portraits of stars at all different life stages. With enough collected data, researchers would be able to see patterns that would help scientists understand how stars behaved at different ages.

One by one, Cannon studied the light from the stars. To the naked eye, a star looks white. But when you send that light through a prism, the prism separates it into its constituent colors. The spectrum is like the star's signature. It reveals clues about its temperature, gases, and metals. Cannon captured these signatures and analyzed them using a magnifying glass similar to a watchmaker's. She dictated her notes to an assistant. As she gathered more and more stellar spectra, other scientists looked for ways to mine it for clues about a star's aging process.

Cannon's classifications were delivered in two big chunks. The first was as a part of the *Henry Draper Catalogue,* a nine-volume star encyclopedia that came out in installments from 1918 to 1925 and included spectral data for 225,300 stars, almost all of them logged by Cannon. Her follow-up effort, a part of the so-called *Henry Draper Extension,* included stars harder to spot. Where magnitude is concerned, the lower the number, the brighter the light. So the first release included stars that could be seen with today's binoculars—stars to magnitude 9. The *Extension* included stars even harder to view, ones classified as magnitude 11. When the *Extension* was published in 1949, it brought the publication's total star count to 359,083.

Cannon didn't invent spectral analysis, but over the years, she certainly streamlined it. Fourteen years after Cannon began work at the Harvard Observatory, her modified classification system became the world standard, still used (in an updated form) today. Cannon's rigorous work transformed the field of astronomy from one based on observation to a full-on scientific discipline, complete with theory and philosophy.

For the decades she spent squinting at spectra, Cannon was given honorary degrees from places like Oxford University in England and awarded prizes like the National Academy of Sciences' Henry Draper Medal. During her lifetime, Cannon was heralded as one of the greatest women alive. "My success, if you would call it that," she said, "lies in the fact that I have kept at my work all these years. It is not genius, or anything like that, it is merely patience."

MARGUERITE PEREY

1909–1975
Chemistry · French

From 1929 to 1939, Marguerite Perey slept next to radioactive material. She worked with radioactive elements at the two-time Nobel Prize winner Marie Curie's Radium Institute and often took her work home. "Home" happened to be a tiny house with bars on the windows, separated from the Radium Institute's lab only by a garden. When she needed time alone, Perey walked her materials across the garden and shut the door. No one else was allowed in. "In those days we took a minimum of precautions," Perey told a reporter decades later. "It was even the thing to scorn dangers of this sort."

Perey started working at the Radium Institute in 1929 at the age of twenty. She had a technician's degree and nothing more. When she was younger, Perey dreamed about becoming a surgeon, but her family didn't have much money. Her father died when she was four, the family business suffered in a stock market crash, and her mother couldn't afford to finance Perey's education. But what she lacked in formal training, she gained in hands-on education. "Under Marie Curie, I suddenly found myself in the midst of the greatest French chemists," Perey remembered. "And there I was, with only a poor diploma." Perey's curiosity and diligence appealed to Curie, who promoted Perey to be her assistant. (To put Curie's belief in Perey in perspective, Curie once turned down the brilliant scientist Lise Meitner, who'd applied to the institute after completing a physics PhD.)

Perey's first assignment was to prepare sources of a radioactive element called actinium for Curie's experiments. Actinium was mixed with other materials—including other radioactive materials related to it—that clouded up the sample. She had to purify it.

Four years in, when she was twenty-four, a sore appeared on Perey's left arm. Because it resembled a burn, Perey's family insisted it was probably just some acid from the lab irritating her skin. Perey had a nagging feeling it wasn't acid doing the damage. A handful of years later, an identical sore surfaced on her right arm. But she put the concern aside. Besides, all this work with actinium was just starting to get interesting.

After purifying actinium for experiments steadily for a decade, Perey knew exactly what to expect from the process. She handled the task with impressive dexterity, improving the purification steps after years of slogging through them. Over time, she performed the task faster and faster. But in the fall of 1938, when measuring a bit of actinium just recently purified, she detected something she'd never seen before; it appeared to be a new radiation.

A few months later, in January 1939, at the age of

twenty-nine, Perey followed that surprising radiation to its source. Her work uncovered a new radioactive element—element 87.

Element 87 filled an empty square in the periodic table. And its addition completed the table's spaces for naturally occurring elements. By the time Perey discovered it, element 87 had been within scientists' grasp for forty years. It escaped detection because no other scientist had been fast enough to spot it. Element 87 is both the most rare and the most unstable of all the natural elements. Only 24.5 grams of the stuff are in Earth's crust at any given time. That's about the weight of ten pennies. It doesn't stick around for long either, so catching it required Perey's singular speed and skill.

Following Curie's example of honoring her country when naming a new element, Perey anointed element 87 "francium." (Curie named the radioactive element she discovered with her husband, Pierre Curie, polonium after Poland, where Curie was born.) Marie Curie died several years before Perey's discovery, but Curie's older daughter, Irène Joliot-Curie, made sure Perey knew her mother would have been proud.

Ten years after she took up residence in her little radioactive cave, Perey moved out victorious. Urged by Joliot-Curie to complete her university education, Perey then took classes at the Sorbonne. She finally earned her PhD in chemistry in 1946. Perey stayed at the Radium Institute for twenty years, climbing the ranks from personal assistant to radiochemist to head of research for the National Center for Scientific Research. In 1949, with Joliot-Curie's blessing, Perey moved to the University of Strasbourg to become the chair of nuclear chemistry, eventually founding her own radiochemistry lab in the tradition of her longtime employer. The lab grew rapidly, hosting a bustling community of some one hundred scientists, students, staff, and, yes, research technicians.

When Perey turned forty, she was finally given an official diagnosis for the ailment that had haunted her for more than fifteen years. She had acquired the sores on her arms from repeat exposure to radioactive materials. Doctors tried to stop the cancer from spreading. By the age of fifty, Perey had undergone twenty surgeries, lost two fingers to the disease, and was in such poor health that her caretakers discouraged her even from reading. As her health declined, Perey was forced to remove herself from the university and her thriving lab.

Though a tragic side effect of an incredible career, Perey's high-profile health problems helped usher in crucial occupational regulations in 1960 that protected others from a similar fate.

In 1962, Perey was the first woman elected to the French Academy of Sciences. It was an honor that, fifty years earlier, her mentor had so desperately wanted. (Curie's admission was defeated by one vote, and a scandal over her candidacy ensued.) Perey was sick then, and getting sicker. As she convalesced in Nice, she reflected on a comment her cousin had made about her scientific fame. "You are the second celebrated person in the family," the cousin said. "In the sixteenth century, one of our ancestors also made a name for himself. He was called Martin the Brawler." Finding a new element was decidedly more dangerous.

MARIE THARP
1920–2006
Cartography · American

Marie Tharp was born in Ypsilanti, Michigan. Her father created soil survey maps for the US Department of Agriculture, and every time he went to a new post, his family went with him. The frequent moving meant that Tharp attended some two dozen schools before she graduated high school. Her father sometimes brought her along on his soil-mapping expeditions.

She earned degrees at three universities: a double major in English and music (with four minors) at Ohio University, a geology degree at the University of Michigan, and a math degree at the University of Tulsa. After college, she had various employment opportunities, but none thrilled her. She found herself "bored as hell" at an oil company. She was unwilling to spend all day squinting through microscopes, and when investigating paleontology, she was put off by how long it would take her to excavate a dinosaur.

Shortly after she was hired by Columbia University in

1948, Tharp began working full-time with geologist Bruce Heezen to map the ocean floor. "I guess I had map-making in my blood," she commented.

But unlike soil, the ocean floor was a mystery. Tharp joked that, for a job to hold her interest, she needed "a once-in-the-history-of-the-world opportunity."

Long ago, the ocean's depths were unreachable by humans. Fishermen imagined that there was no bottom below their boats. In the years leading up to 1851, the seafloor was thought to be mostly flat, a smooth sloped basin that swooped from continent to continent, slowly filling with sediment at its edges until the bottom gained enough ground to emerge from the salt water. In the mid-nineteenth century, the ocean was imagined as a "great sea-gash . . . a scene the most rugged, grand, and imposing. The very ribs of the solid earth."

By 1910, the idea that the world's continents were once connected was raised and quickly buried when one of the world's most prominent geologists called the theory "poppycock." After that, everyone else considering the mysteries of the ocean floor fell into line. Everyone except Marie Tharp, that is. When she brought the possibility to the attention of her research partner, Heezen, in 1952, resurrecting the theory of continental drift was "a form of scientific heresy." The suggestion did not go over well. Tharp and Heezen fought. She insisted. He discounted it as "girl talk." And for a few years, they put the discussion aside.

When mapping the ocean floor, Tharp and Heezen initially worked from a US Navy data set. During World War II, navy ships were outfitted with instruments that measured echoes. When a ship sent a sonic ping downward, a stylus would move across a piece of paper on board like a needle on a record. When the ping returned, bouncing off the ocean floor and returning to the ship, the stylus would burn a hole in the paper with an electric spark, marking the ocean floor's depth. The recording process happened continuously, providing Heezen and Tharp with the largest data haul of ocean-floor-depth measurements available at the time. The technology had a little snag, however. When soldiers opened the ship's refrigerator, the electric power shut off—and so did the instrument's ability to measure accurately. "When that happened," said Tharp, "no echo returned and the sounder recorded depths [as] bottomless as the crew's appetite."

By 1952, the research team had collected tens of thousands of measurements—a few drops in the bucket. Even at that number, most of the ocean floor was still uncharted.

Heezen collected the data and Tharp mapped it. Spread out over drafting tables set up at Columbia University's Lamont Geological Observatory in Palisades, New York, Tharp weaved depth measurements together to create three-dimensional maps. She'd position the map's key over the places in the ocean that didn't have any data.

Meanwhile, Heezen hired a fine arts graduate from Boston to work on a parallel project for Bell Laboratories. Heezen asked the graduate to plot underwater earthquake epicenters. Bell Labs wanted to know where the currents that ripped apart the company's cables originated. Heezen insisted that the student use the same scale map that Tharp was using to map the ocean floor.

Tharp and the earthquake artist switched on the light table. Tharp placed the ocean floor first, and the fine arts grad added his earthquake map on top. Together, the maps revealed something incredible. Like keys on a flute, the earthquakes lined up along the Mid-Atlantic Ridge—a mountain range that stretches from north to south through the Atlantic Ocean.

And there it was. Tharp was convinced the continental drift was real. It would be two more years before Heezen believed her.

In 1959, continental drift got a sizable publicity boost, thanks to Jacques Cousteau, who along with almost everybody else wasn't a supporter of the theory. However, Cousteau was curious, so he sailed to the ridge, put a camera on a sled, and dragged it near the seafloor. "He took beautiful movies of big black cliffs in blue water, which he showed at the first International Ocean Congress in New York in 1959," remembered Tharp. "It helped a lot of people believe in our rift valley."

But Heezen was stubborn. He and Tharp had grand fights in which they hurled map weights and kicked trash cans. But for all their fighting, they were very close. When up against others, they formed a united front.

Although Heezen eventually came around, others did not. Heezen's supervisor was so furious about the pair's conclusion that he fired Tharp and made sure Heezen, who was tenured, had a wicked hard time carrying out his work.

Tharp was not defined by an office drafting table. Even after she lost her official position, she worked from home,

installing a guard dog named Inky to protect against un-
friendly former coworkers. Fortunately, Heezen had
enough contacts to continue the ocean floor exploration,
and finally, after years of being told she had to stay home,
Tharp was cleared to join the project's research vessel.

The partnership between Tharp and Heezen filled in 70
percent of the globe and completely changed the field of
geophysics. In her own words, Tharp says, "Establishing
the rift valley and the mid-ocean ridge that went all the
way around the world for 40,000 miles—that was something important. You could only do that once. You can't
find anything bigger than that, at least on this planet."

YVONNE BRILL

1924–2013
Engineering · Canadian

When Brill was four years old, Amelia Earhart became the first woman to fly solo across the Atlantic. To the young Brill, finding freedom through flight looked extraordinary. It was nothing like what she saw growing up in Manitoba, Canada, as the third and youngest child of Belgian immigrant parents who hadn't made it through high school. But no matter. One heroine taking flight was sufficient to prove that there were faraway places to go and extraordinary things to do.

At ten, she passed the University of Manitoba on a streetcar and decided she'd attend. So she worked hard in school to get there. In high school, Brill's physics teacher told her that women couldn't amount to anything. When she applied to the University of Manitoba, the engineering department told her that it wouldn't admit women. Never mind that; she went to the university, and by the time she graduated in mathematics and chemistry at age twenty, Brill was at

the top of her class. Soon after, she secured a one-way ticket
to Los Angeles. "I didn't really discuss it with my parents,"
Brill said later in an interview, laughing. "I just went ahead
and got all the paperwork together and left."

During the day, Brill worked as a mathematician contributing to the design of the first American satellite at Douglas Aircraft. At night, she pursued a master's in chemistry
at the University of Southern California. In the mid-1940s,
there was likely only one woman in the United States
working in rocket science. That woman was Yvonne Brill.
After several years of mathematics, including figuring out
the trajectories of different rocket stage sizes, using just a
slide rule, Brill found that the purely theoretical work at
Douglas Aircraft made her restless. She wanted to see her
work actually take off, but to do it, she needed to change
specialties. Brill considered a career in chemistry, where
she had already earned a graduate degree, but ultimately
decided against it because of the field's heavy discrimination against women. "There was just no question," she
remembered in an interview with the Society of Women
Engineers. "Whereas engineering, as an individual of one,
they weren't about to make rules to block your progress,
because that was too much trouble." She made the switch.

Brill first worked as a chemical engineer in Southern
California before moving to the East Coast, where she
worked on turbojet engine cycles and chemical manufacturing performance calculations. At the time, electric
propulsion systems were, as she called them, "the cat's
meow"—both new and one hundred times more powerful
than what was then capable with chemical propulsion. But
there was still a lot to learn.

Brill started thinking about a particular, crucial moment—precisely when a satellite is injected into orbit. Like golfers lining up putts, satellites often need to make little adjustments once they're placed into orbit. The chemical propulsion system at the time was overly complicated, and electric systems needed too much power.

Years earlier, Brill had studied German rockets and had become fascinated with the potential of their chemical propulsion systems. So she began by "looking at the performance and trying to decide what areas of the periodic table one could put emphasis on to get higher performance fuels." Too busy with her day job to devote any on-the-clock hours to a passion project, Brill worked on weekends and late into the night, hunkering down at her kitchen table with pencils, yellow notepads, and a slide rule. Finally confident that she was onto something after examining the ammonia, hydrogen, and nitrogen produced under different conditions, Brill recruited someone with enough skill to check her work. "I never was afraid to risk my job to further ideas that I thought should be adopted, that were good technical ideas, that maybe somebody considered were a little bit far out. But as long as I knew technically I was on the right—or had the confidence that I was technically on the right path, I'd push it." What she discovered was a more fuel-efficient chemical propulsion thruster that helped satellites carry more-substantial payloads and remain in orbit for longer periods of time.

Her electrothermal hydrazine thruster was still being used in satellites when she died in 2013. It may have been Brill's best-known contribution to rocket science, but it was by no means her only one. Over the course of her career, which took place in the United States and England, Brill worked on the Nova rockets that took America to the moon, the first weather satellite, the first satellite stationed in the upper atmosphere, the *Mars Observer*, and the engine for the space shuttle. For this work, she was awarded the Resnik Challenger Medal by the Society of Women Engineers, the Wyld Propulsion Award from the American Institute of Aeronautics and Astronautics (AIAA), and the National Medal of Technology and Innovation, among others. "She truly represented the best of what American aerospace engineering and system development should be—a pioneering spirit coupled to a clear vision of what the future of an entire area of systems should be, with the ingenuity and genius necessary to make that vision a reality," said AIAA president Mike Griffin in 2013.

With the Society of Women Engineers, Brill spent decades both encouraging women to go into math and sciences and encouraging institutions to give female engineers the recognition they deserved. In return, the society gave her access to a network of women all carving out a then unconventional career.

There's a story Brill liked to tell about a visitor from another company coming into RCA, where she worked at the time, to give a talk. During his presentation, the visitor asked how many propulsion engineers worked at the company. Brill was the only one. Horrified, the visitor explained that his company employed seventy-five. An RCA program manager then piped up: "We believe in quality, not quantity."

SALLY RIDE

1951–2012
Astrophysics · American

Before becoming the first American woman in space, Sally
Ride got a PhD in astrophysics from Stanford University and subjected herself to five years of astronaut training at NASA. Navy test pilots took her on gut-dropping,
600-mile-per-hour flights 39,000 feet in the air. (Her flight
instructor called her the best student he'd ever had.) Ride
became an expert at maneuvering a 900-pound robotic arm
that would be used to pluck satellites from the sky. She
became fluent in switches and circuits, getting to know
the 1,800 or so on the orbiter's control panel. Ride en-
dured long days of training with singular focus. In another
life, Ride would have been a professional tennis player
or a Nobel Prize winner—both were within the realm of
possibility—but in this one, she reached the top of a stack
of 8,079 other space program applicants. She was an ambitious scientist and, as soon as her 1983 mission was announced, an instant sensation.

Ride landed on magazine covers and in talk-show opening monologues. After years of impossible hurdles thrown
up by NASA to prevent women from flying (no, but seriously: the agency's push for women and people of color
was summarized as a "near total failure" in 1973 by the
person in charge of it), Ride became living proof that gender wasn't the characteristic that would get one booted
from the application pool.

She handled space training with ease. Making it through
the gauntlet of inane press questions may have been more
of a challenge. *Would or wouldn't she wear a bra in zero
gravity? Did she cry over her mistakes?* Questions about how
her gender would affect the flight were typically answered
with some flatly delivered variation of the following: "One
thing I probably share with everyone else in the astronaut
office is composure." Or, as she reminded one reporter,
"Weightlessness is a great equalizer."

Ride was unflappable. Her strategy the morning of her
first launch in 1983 was to approach her preparations as if
they were mechanical obligations, so as not to get too over-
whelmed by the excitement. The astronaut had a knack
for tamping down emotion—even if it meant taming the
ultimate thrill. When reporters asked, *Why did you want to
go into space? What was it like looking back at Earth?* Ride's
answers were sometimes flat. *I didn't dream about going to
space, I'm not sure why I applied,* and *I can't describe what it
was like to look back on Earth.* To say the view from space
was not the same as seeing a picture of it was, at least in
the beginning, as eloquent as she got.

Ride was better with the concrete, like learning a task or

memorizing a text. During her time as an undergraduate at Stanford, while majoring in both English and physics, Ride and her doubles tennis partner playfully battled each other over who could more seamlessly work obscure Shakespeare quotes into a conversation. As she rose through the academic ranks, Ride recalled her physics adviser saying, "Well! A girl physics major! I've been waiting to see what you'd look like—I haven't seen one for years!" As would become a common theme, Ride was the only one.

Ride went up in the space shuttle twice. The image of her floating through the cabin with a halo of curly brown hair, snagging a bag of cashews, inspired tremendous hope for girls dreaming of going into science. Her presence brought some admirers to tears and compelled others to act.

When an advertisement for college financial aid services displayed a boy in an astronaut outfit dreaming about his future, Ride's father sent the company a strongly worded letter complaining about the "unconscious (I assume) bias we have in education. . . . As a parent of the first US woman astronaut, I know firsthand that girls also aspire to math and science and we should encourage her to 'get America's future off the ground.' "

Ride was more than just the first woman in space. She served as an essential voice of reason—twice—when NASA most needed it.

On January 28, 1986, space shuttle *Challenger* exploded seventy-three seconds after liftoff. Seven of Ride's colleagues died in the accident. Space flight up until then had always been the stuff of dreams. But NASA's push for rapid-fire missions at the expense of safety sacrificed lives. The agency needed to figure out what went wrong and how it could recover.

Of the thirteen people brought in to sit on a presidential commission to review the accident, Ride was the only current NASA representative. She was also responsible for gathering some of the most shocking information regarding the agency's missteps. Ride helped hold her employer accountable. The report concluded that NASA had forced through too many flights, ignored warnings that weather conditions might put astronauts in danger, and was entirely too cavalier about sending humans into space. Ride told a reporter that, considering what had just happened, she wouldn't feel safe getting on a space flight just then.

The explosion grounded the shuttle program for two years while NASA regrouped. With more rigorous safety measures put in place, the organization needed to map out a plan to win back the public's trust while also making important decisions about the kinds of missions that would take the agency forward. NASA put Ride in charge of coming up with a refreshed list of mission recommendations.

For a year, Ride tapped young NASA employees to brainstorm the agency's next move. In her final report, she weighed four recommendations: sending humans to Mars, exploring the solar system, creating a space station on the moon, and the one she was most passionate about, organizing a mission to planet Earth. Internally, the organization favored big projects that ignited the imagination. The longtime NASA heavyweights wanted a mission to Mars; Ride argued for an approach more beneficial to the planet.

Mission to planet Earth's goal was to use space technology to understand Earth as a total system, to learn how manmade and natural shifts affect the environment. "This initiative," she wrote, "directly addresses the problems that will be facing humanity in the coming decades, and its continuous scientific return will produce results which are of major significance to all the residents of the planet." At a meeting of the Senate Committee on Commerce, Science, and Transportation, a senator asked Ride to prove how her preferred mission would be more than just "a better weather report." Following the meeting's conclusion, the same senator gushed that the initiative was "the most challenging and exciting concept that this committee has seen in quite some time."

Finally, Ride had an answer to those questions about seeing Earth from space. The astrophysicist in her saw a fragile planet. Her greatest legacy is convincing NASA that Earth is worth trying to protect.

HEALTH AND MEDICINE

Twenty years ago, it was common for kids to get the chicken pox. One kid in a class would get the red spots and get sick and then a whole daisy chain of students would find themselves spotted and itching. When a child was infected, often bothersome blisters would pop up all over his or her body that would last for days and occasionally weeks. And then researchers developed a chicken pox vaccine to spare children and adults from the annoying—and sometimes dangerous—illness.

Medical breakthroughs like this happen all the time. Imagine how many we've made in the last twenty years, fifty years, one hundred years. Now imagine what it would be like without them.

When Ellen Swallow Richards began her career as a chemist in the second half of the nineteenth century, there weren't any organizations in Massachusetts, where she worked, that made sure water was safe for drinking.

Think about that for a minute. Sewage, by-products from factories—no one monitoring the water to check that the liquid people drank was free from nasty contaminants . . . until Ellen Swallow Richards.

And it gets worse. The public had little knowledge about basic food safety—things we'd find essential today, such as how to prepare food so that it doesn't make us sick. Furthermore, illnesses like typhoid and leprosy, and conditions like lead poisoning and malnutrition, still popped up in the developed world. These dangerous problems are now the stuff of historical novels and fiction: a stomach bug that kills you, melting skin, a decline in mental function, and delayed physical development. But then? Staying healthy was a constant game of parasite and disease dodgeball.

Scientists like Ellen Swallow Richards, Alice Ball, Virginia Apgar, and Elsie Widdowson stepped in to help, occasionally experimenting on themselves to get a deeper understanding of a problem and its solution. Elsie Widdowson, for instance, injected herself with vitamins and minerals. Luckily, we can celebrate these women's accomplishments without duplicating their methods.

With perseverance and creativity, these doctors and scientists succeeded, making crucially important discoveries that continue to help us live healthier lives, starting from the very first moments we're born.

ELLEN SWALLOW RICHARDS

1842–1911
Chemistry · American

A glass of water can perfectly quench thirst. It's important to note that drinking water was not always clean. Before 1887, water quality standards in Massachusetts did not exist. We didn't have water treatment plants operated by cities, as we have today. To take a sip of water in Cambridge, Massachusetts, in the late nineteenth century could put you at risk of consuming either industrial waste or municipal sewage.

Ellen Swallow Richards hoped to make drinking water cleaner and safer for people. Richards was an instructor at the Massachusetts Institute of Technology's newly founded laboratory of sanitary chemistry, where she supervised the collection and analysis of some twenty thousand water samples. The design of her experiments set the standard for similar studies by other scientists. What Richards learned allowed her to make assumptions about the quality of the water in the area, as well as the drinking water conditions globally. Richards's water quality studies were an important contribution to science and public health.

Richards was the first woman to work as a professional chemist in the United States. Richards believed that science could do an extraordinary amount to improve our daily lives. To tackle problems like water contamination, scientists and government have a crucial role to play in keeping our tap water clean and safe. But Richards also believed that by extending sanitation standards and basic science into the home, researchers would see vast improvements in the public's health. (The field of sanitation engineering—that is, the job of designing the facilities and systems to get communities clean water and remove human waste—sprouted in the late 1800s, thanks largely to Richards's work.) In addition to being one of the earliest voices in ecology, a field that studies the relationship between living things and their environment, Richards is also known for founding another major area of study: home economics.

But let's back up a bit. Before the water samples or home economics, in 1870, Richards was the first woman to be admitted to the Massachusetts Institute of Technology (MIT). MIT let her attend tuition-free as a sort of insurance policy. Should anyone affiliated with the university complain about her, MIT could claim she wasn't really a student and "that her admission did not establish a precedent for the general admission of females." At the time, Richards was oblivious to the reasoning behind her status at the university. She later admitted, "Had I realized upon what basis I was taken, I would not have gone."

Richards earned both a bachelor's and a master's degree at Vassar College and then a second bachelor's degree in chemistry from MIT. But when she started work on her PhD, MIT stopped her from getting an advanced degree. The university simply wasn't ready to bestow the honor on a woman.

Richards did not believe she was an exceptional case—a member of a rare group of women earning the same academic degrees as men. Because she was able to get a good education (or most of one), she wanted to make sure to extend these opportunities to other women wanting to do the same. However, MIT still wasn't officially open to women. With funding and initiative provided by the Women's Education Association of Boston, Richards spearheaded the creation of a parallel science program for women on the MIT campus. Opened in 1876, the Women's Laboratory at MIT was a place for budding scientists to conduct research and take classes. The lab was made up of two rooms flanked by big windows. Passersby saw a rare spectacle: women studying industrial chemistry, mineralogy, and physiology. In a report Richards wrote on the program she started, she revealed her feelings about being able to share science with other women: "I have felt the greatest satisfaction in opening the treasures of our storehouse."

Her influence quickly spread beyond her charges in the Women's Laboratory. Richards also wrote letters to women who enrolled in correspondence courses. The courses were part of an effort to increase access to education, initiated by the Society to Encourage Studies at Home. The idea was that Richards would teach her distant pupils science, but her pupils soon sought her advice for a myriad of problems. In their letters, women reported conditions at home were bleak. Women were overworked, and ill health was a common problem.

The concerns of her faraway students spurred Richards to act. She decided to incorporate science-based advice into her prescriptions for improving life in the home. Richards began talking to her pen pals about eating a more balanced diet, preparing healthy foods, exercising regularly, and wearing comfortable clothes (corsets were mighty uncomfortable, yet still in fashion at the time).

In ironic testament to its success, the Women's Laboratory shut down in 1883, when women were finally admitted to MIT's standard set of science classes. Shortly thereafter, Richards began her groundbreaking work on water sanitation and took a position as a chemist and water analyst for the Massachusetts State Board of Health. At the same time, Richards formulated a plan to deliver science to women.

In 1890, Richards's efforts to address the lack of information about nutritious, inexpensive, and safe food preparation resulted in the opening of a kitchen that both served food and provided hands-on education for the public. The kitchen started supplying nutritious meals to schoolchildren four years later. (The program predated Michelle Obama's healthy school lunch initiative by 116 years.)

Richards also advocated for domestic science to be taught in public schools. Her efforts rolled out slowly, but gradually they became a movement. Richards published books and gave speeches, and in 1908, the American Home Economics Association was founded with Richards as its president. Home economics became a major conduit to bringing women into science at the university level.

Richards had the extraordinary vision to see how science's influence could extend in all directions, from sanitation to conservation to education, home, health, and happiness. All it took was knowledge and, yes, twenty thousand water samples.

ANNA WESSELS WILLIAMS

1863–1954
Bacteriology · American

Anna Wessels Williams believed working with others was essential, but she also used every moment of her free time to go alone in stunt planes, teetering between the stomach-dropping danger of flight and the sublime feeling of gliding where so few others could. On the ground, she piled up speeding tickets, the allure of zipping around other cars apparently too tempting to resist when she was driving. Williams was also alone in the New York City Department of Health's diagnostic laboratory when she made one of the lab's greatest discoveries. In 1894, she isolated a strain of the infectious disease diphtheria. That strain became crucial in developing higher yields of an antitoxin needed for fighting the infection.

Today, diphtheria is under control, but when Anna Wessels Williams was working alone, it had reached "near-epidemic levels." The disease hitched a ride on spittle transferred from one person to the next during a cough or during conversation. At first, diphtheria gave those infected a fever or chills, but when it really settled in, it could wreak havoc on the heart and nervous system. In the late 1800s, children were dying. Children living in poverty were disproportionately at risk.

Emil von Behring had discovered an antitoxin for diphtheria in 1890. It was a breakthrough that would earn von Behring the Nobel Prize in Medicine in 1901. But discovering a therapy that works in a lab is different from being able to deploy it globally. Producing it on a large scale has its own challenges. Von Behring's antitoxin needed a toxin to activate it. In the four years following his discovery, scientists had trouble making enough of the therapy to fight the infection. The disease continued to leap from person to person, killing thousands of children every year.

Under the guidance of William H. Park at the New York City Department of Health's diagnostic laboratory, Anna Williams got to work on finding a strain of the bacteria that could bring forth a powerful toxin to activate the antitoxin, and in high enough volume to produce it for lots and lots of people. She had a breakthrough while Park was away on vacation. Williams isolated a strain of bacteria that could generate a toxin five hundred times more potent than what was previously available. A more potent toxin provoked more of the antitoxin, which meant that there would be more treatment to go around.

The strain was named Park-Williams No. 8. Gracious about her boss's inclusion, Williams said she was "happy to have the honor of having my name thus associated with Dr. Park." Williams recognized the necessity of collaboration in research. After all, Williams's own experiments were bolstered by von Behring's initial breakthrough. But over time, Park-Williams No. 8 proved too many syllables for the people who worked with it; informally, it became known as Park 8. Just like that, Williams's pioneering work was clipped from view.

Name recognition wasn't why Williams got into science; she wasn't concerned with how many strains of bacteria her name was attached to. Her sense of purpose originated from addressing a medical need. Where real-world good was concerned, Park 8 succeeded spectacularly. Since the new strain increased the antitoxin's availability and slashed cost, Williams's work was instrumental in slowing down the spread of disease. Within a year of her discovery, the diphtheria antitoxin went into mass production. To address the staggering demand, mass quantities of the preparation were shipped to physicians in the United States and England without charge.

Williams's decision to go into medical science originated from a time when she witnessed one bad event spin out of control. In 1887, her sister nearly died during childbirth, and her sister's baby died before delivery. Williams believed that the devastating event would have been at least partially avoidable had the attending physician been more thoroughly trained. The incident gave Williams resolve. She would battle such medical ignorance with her own education.

Almost immediately, Williams quit her job as a schoolteacher in order to enroll in classes at the Women's Medical College of the New York Infirmary. She found this new study thrilling. She recounted excitedly, "I was starting on

a way that had been practically untrod by a woman. My belief at the time in human individuality, regardless of sex, race, religion or any factor other than ability was at its strongest. I believed, therefore, that females should have equal opportunities with males to develop their powers to the utmost." By 1891, she'd earned her medical degree.

At the NYC Department of Health, opportunities to tackle nasty diseases appeared almost immediately. That diphtheria breakthrough? It happened in 1894, in Williams's first year at the organization, when she was still just a volunteer. The Department of Health added Williams to the payroll the following year and gave her a title: assistant bacteriologist.

Creative and fearless, Williams took a sabbatical in Paris in 1896 to research scarlet fever at the Pasteur Institute. There she was met with a culture of deep secrecy, where discussion of time-sensitive research was strictly prohibited and research tools, such as cadavers, were not to be shared. She hoped to do for scarlet fever what she'd done for diphtheria, but her research wasn't fruitful.

Williams redeemed the trip by studying rabies, a fatal disease that is spread between warm-blooded animals through saliva. It is a worry to people because wild animals infected with rabies can spread the disease by biting humans. In Paris, Williams looked into the problems of diagnosis and prevention that the disease posed. When it was time for her to return to the United States, she took a culture of the rabies vaccine with her. In her lab at the NYC Department of Health, she cared for the culture, coaxing it to grow. Eventually, she had enough to produce vaccinations for fifteen people. Following Williams's interest, the

United States promoted a major initiative aimed at producing the vaccine.

Having handed off one part of the problem, Williams flipped back to studying rabies detection. The disease was maddeningly difficult to diagnose, and by the time scientists concretely pinpointed it in a patient, the opportunity for a vaccine had already expired. Rabies affects the nervous system and brain, so Williams started to look for flags the virus plants inside the body that might be used for early detection. And sure enough: Williams noticed that the virus was manhandling the structure of cells in the brain. It was major news, but Williams lost the headline again. While meticulously checking and double-checking her results, an Italian physician named Adelchi Negri independently discovered the cells. He beat her to the pages of a scholarly journal. Those rabies-affected cells are now called Negri bodies, named after the scientist who published his results first.

After rabies, Williams worked her way through research on venereal disease, eye infections, influenza, pneumonia, meningitis, and smallpox. Early on, her studies were powered by the drive "to find out about the what, why, when and where and how of the mysteries of life," she explained. "This trait had increased with the years, and finally had become a passion."

In 1934, Williams and nearly one hundred other workers over seventy years old were forced to retire by New York City mayor Fiorello La Guardia. But word of her important contributions to bacteriology made it to Mayor La Guardia, who called her "a scientist of international repute."

ALICE HAMILTON

1869–1970

Bacteriology · American

Alice Hamilton's numerous professional successes fell at the intersection of science and social issues. Although she earned a degree in medicine from the University of Michigan, gaining further training in bacteriology and pathology in Germany at the University of Leipzig and the University of Munich, she didn't think herself capable of becoming anything more than a "fourth-rate bacteriologist." But what she lacked in bravado, she made up in her dedication to problems both "human and practical": typhoid outbreaks, lead poisoning, and the widespread horror of occupational disease.

Hamilton was never afraid to get her hands dirty. Take her approach to the epidemic of typhoid fever that broke out in Chicago in 1902. The area most severely affected was the one directly around Hamilton's residence. With her training in pathology and bacteriology, a friend figured that if Hamilton could root out the outbreak's cause, the city could formulate a solution.

First, Hamilton investigated the water and milk supplies, but neither explained why the nineteenth ward specifically was hit so hard. Next, she surveyed the neighborhood, hoping that visual clues might lead her to the answer. "As I prowled about the streets and the ramshackle wooden tenement houses, I saw the outdoor privies (toilets—forbidden by law but flourishing nevertheless), some of them in backyards below the level of the street and overflowing in heavy rains," she explained. "The wretched water closets indoors, one for four or more families, filthy and with the plumbing out of order because nobody was responsible for cleaning or repairs; and swarms of flies everywhere." And there it was: the flies.

One way typhoid, which causes humans to become very ill, is transferred is by exposure to sewage contaminated with the bacteria. Perhaps, Hamilton thought, the flies were gobbling up the diseased human waste and then landing on uncovered food and milk, spreading the disease.

Hamilton put her theory to the test by collecting the pests from kitchens and both indoor and outdoor bathrooms. Sure enough, the flies were carriers of typhoid bacillus. Hamilton's findings squared well with previous observations made during the Spanish-American War, and they also explained why wealthier people—those with reliable plumbing and screened-in eating areas—weren't having the same problems. Presented to the Chicago Medical Society, Hamilton's paper won lots of attention, prompting a total reorganization of the city's health department, including the addition of an expert dedicated to inspecting tenement housing.

Although the outcome was positive, Hamilton's explanation was incorrect. As she later found out, the real cause of the typhoid outbreak was one actively covered up by the board of health; a sewage spill had contaminated the water supply in the nineteenth ward for three straight days. "For years," admitted Hamilton, "although I did my best to lay the ghosts of those flies, they haunted me and mortified me, compelling me again and again to explain to deeply impressed audiences that the dramatic story . . . had little foundation in fact."

But uncovering these truths—no matter how buried in muck—was what made Hamilton so exceptionally effective at assessing unsafe environments. Remarkably skilled at gathering information from sources that didn't want to provide it, Hamilton was able to make tremendous headway in unsafe industries by asking workers, *Why do you keep a job that's clearly killing you?* She conducted interviews in their home, where she figured workers would be comfortable and forthcoming. During one such visit, Hamilton asked a man suffering from lead poisoning why he continued to show up to work. House payments and a family stopped him from quitting, he said. The plants often preferred to hire married men. Hamilton suspected the choice was calculated. Out of an obligation to support their families, workers were less likely to quit, even when lead was causing colic, convulsions, and weight loss.

In 1910, Hamilton's focus shifted full-time to health in the workplace, when she was asked to serve as the managing director of the occupational disease commission in Illinois—the first commission of its kind in the country.

The task was to survey the state's "poisonous occupations," to figure out what kinds of plants were exposing workers to harmful substances like carbon monoxide, arsenic, and turpentine, and to assess how many plants existed. The team split up according to the noxious substances they would study. Hamilton took lead. At the start of the project, the government knew neither what industries manufactured with lead nor how pervasive its ill effects were.

Hamilton dug in, starting with the most obvious lead-using industries and hoping those inquiries would draw her nearer to ones she didn't know about. She and her team approached the project with a detective's scrutiny by visiting plants, interviewing doctors and industry leaders, and combing through hospital records for telltale signs of patients with lead poisoning. Her inquiries shook out a long list of processes that required lead, including freight-car seals, coffin trim, glass polishing, and "tin foil" cigar wrappers (*tin foil* turned out to be a misnomer). Hamilton found buildings dilapidated and improperly vented, with lead dust clouding the air even around those workers who didn't produce it. In one plant, an astonishing 40 percent of employees had gone to the hospital for becoming "leaded."

By 1919, Hamilton was the foremost expert on industrial health in the United States. So when Harvard decided to expand their curriculum to include public health, Hamilton noted, "I was about the only candidate available." Hired as an assistant professor of industrial medicine, Hamilton became Harvard Medical School's first female faculty member, predating the arrival of female medical students by twenty-six years. (Her appointment came with three stipulations: she was not to set foot in the Harvard Club, she was not to claim faculty-reserved tickets for football games, and she was not permitted to participate in commencement ceremonies.) The appointment caused quite a sensation, but Hamilton recalled the welcome as warm.

While working half-time at Harvard and half-time doing fieldwork, Hamilton investigated carbon monoxide poisoning for the US Department of Labor. She also looked into the virulent effects of aniline dyes, mercury, volatile solvents, and other toxic products. Her reputation spread. General Electric tapped her as a medical consultant, the President's Research Committee on Social Trends appointed her as a member, and she was brought onto the Health Committee of the League of Nations and the Public Health Service of Soviet Russia to consult on industrial hygiene.

In her memoir, *Exploring the Dangerous Trades,* Hamilton expressed pleasure in leading messy, deleterious, misinformed industries to a healthier future. "No young doctor nowadays can hope for work as exciting and rewarding. Everything I discovered was new and most of it was really valuable." The industries to which Hamilton applied her unique expertise underwent dramatic change as a result. After her yearlong study of lead in Illinois, the state passed a law that compensated workers for harmful exposure to noxious gases, dusts, and fumes. The law set off a systemic change. Because employers began to insure against such health-related claims, insurance companies responded by pushing for workplace reforms. By 1937, most of the states carrying the country's largest industrial burdens had adopted legislative requirements that workers had to be paid for being poisoned.

By knocking on the doors of a city's poorest residences and applying pathology to the problems she observed, Hamilton was able to record solid evidence of occupational illness. Her pioneering determination paved the way for more social change.

ALICE BALL

1892–1916
Chemistry · American

Leprosy ravages the skin. It attacks the mucous membranes in the eyes, nose, and throat. And it goes after the peripheral nerves, located outside the brain and the spinal cord. The ability to feel pain disappears, and chunks of skin develop into lesions. The damage is caused by a relative of tuberculosis. Although leprosy—now called Hansen's disease—is not as contagious as most people think, to this day, doctors still don't understand how it travels from person to person.

Jack London, the author of *The Call of the Wild*, called Kalaupapa, a tile of land on the Hawaiian island of Molokai, "The pit of hell, the most cursed place on earth." On three sides, the area is surrounded by ocean. On the fourth, it's fenced in by a sheer two-thousand-foot cliff. It wasn't easy to get in. It was even harder to get out.

The area's occupants were sent to this remote area because they were struck with what was called the living death. Beginning in 1866 and lasting for eighty years, some eight thousand people with leprosy were ripped from their homes, arrested, and relocated to Kalaupapa, never to be seen again. For families, these departures were treated like deaths. A funeral was held, property was distributed, and families mourned the loss of a person still living. Sufferers were considered dangerous disease spreaders and, without a cure, a lost cause.

For hundreds of years, the closest thing to leprosy medication was an oil that came from the seeds of the chaulmoogra tree. People smeared it on their skin, swallowed it, and even injected it, but each delivery method was problematic. Rubbing it on like lotion didn't have any negative effects, but it also didn't do much good. The oil's acrid taste made swallowing it nauseating. When it was injected, the treatment just sat under the skin in a lump, getting along exactly as you'd expect oil and water to. Not well. (An adult male body is about 60 percent water.) The injected oil became a subcutaneous snail; as it traveled, it burned.

Researchers were looking for a stronger solution. A surgeon named Harry T. Hollmann, working out of Kalihi Hospital in Honolulu, just an island over from Kalaupapa, took particular interest in leprosy patients because when they fell ill, he was one of the doctors who treated them. Chaulmoogra oil was introduced in the Hawaiian Islands in 1879, and Hollmann was intrigued by its storied properties. Some patients really did seem to show improvement, but the benefits, as a whole, were scattershot. (One reason for the uneven therapeutic effects was that not all oils peddled as chaulmoogra were the real deal.)

Hollmann was one of many scientists all over the world looking for a better way to whip the chaulmoogra oil into an injectable therapy for leprosy. The project needed a chemist, and that chemist was Alice Ball.

Ball was in her early twenties and an instructor at the College of Hawaii when Hollmann reached out. She had completed her undergraduate education at the University of Washington. She earned a degree in chemistry in 1912 and then another in pharmacy in 1914. She lived in Hawaii as a child, when her parents moved from Washington State to Honolulu to take advantage of the warmer climate, hoping that it would ease the grip of arthritis on Ball's grandfather. The relocation lasted a single year. When her grandfather died, the family returned to Seattle.

After her studies at the University of Washington, Ball published an article in the *Journal of the American Chemical Society* and then returned to Hawaii for a master's in chemistry. In 1915, she was both the first woman and the first African American to earn a graduate degree at the College of Hawaii. Ball continued on as an instructor at the school.

By the time she began her work with Hollmann, the chaulmoogra oil had already stumped many of his contemporaries. When a treatment is not water-soluble, often scientists will coax it into its salt form, which can be absorbed by the body. But in the case of chaulmoogra oil, the salts would be so big that they would act like soaps, which could badly damage a body's red blood cells. Ball had to blaze her own way to a solution.

Untreated, the oil was closer to honey than to the liquid oil you cook with. Ball had to figure out a way to thin it out. First, Ball managed to manipulate the oil so that it would form a better relationship with water. The goal was for the oil to be absorbed by the body rather than repelled. She treated the oil's fatty acids with an alcohol and a catalyst to kick-start the reaction to create a less viscous chemical compound.

With a bit more finessing, Ball became the first person in the world to successfully prepare a form of the oil that could be injected and absorbed by the body. In her formulation, there were no abscesses or bitter taste, and patients were able to get some relief. Ball, who fit the research in around her teaching schedule, made the breakthrough when she was just twenty-three years old.

Soon after solving one big problem, Ball was hit with another. At age twenty-four, in the middle of instructing a class, Ball may have mistakenly inhaled some chlorine gas. This time the reaction did not go in her favor. Chlorine interacts with water in the body, turning it to acid. Ball was flown back to Seattle in a last-ditch effort to save her life, but ultimately the damage was too great and she died.

In 1918, two years after her death, an article in the *Journal of the American Medical Association* reported that seventy-eight patients with leprosy admitted to the Kalihi Hospital had been discharged—not back to Kalaupapa but to their original homes. Ball's chaulmoogra oil preparation worked. For four years, not a single new patient was exiled to Kalaupapa, and other leper populations were let out on parole—thanks to a gender, race, and chaulmoogra oil barrier-breaking chemist.

HELEN TAUSSIG

1898–1986

Medicine · American

Helen Taussig studied the heart, but she could not hear it. That *thu-thud, thu-thud* sound started fading when she was around thirty, the most fundamental indicator of life eluding her failing ears. As a stopgap, she modified her stethoscope with an amplifier. But as her hearing deteriorated further, Taussig began feeling for the heart's beat instead of listening for it. She read the rhythm like Morse code, interpreting the signal for an organ's abnormalities. Supplemented with blood pressure results and electrocardiogram images, which monitor the electrical signals in a person's heart, Taussig pieced together a series of clues in order to come to a plausible diagnosis. She called this triangulation of evidence and monitoring "the crossword puzzle."

Taussig was a founder of pediatric cardiology—a specialist in studying the hearts of children. When she entered the field around 1930, it was considered a dead-end specialty. This was before surgeons performed open-heart surgery, so physicians could diagnose heart abnormalities, but they couldn't do anything substantial to treat them. Pediatric patients with heart problems routinely died. When they did, the autopsy would provide the crossword puzzle's final clue.

Without a clear understanding of where her research would lead, Taussig gathered data about her patients' health and heart to formulate her diagnoses. Gathering data wasn't a solution to the heart abnormalities she saw in patients, but after more than a decade of observation and testing, Taussig amassed the most comprehensive catalog of congenital heart defects and their indicators ever compiled. Still, she couldn't help her patients recover.

Taussig had plenty of experience in perseverance. Her mother died when she was eleven, and as a child, she worked extra hard in her classes to compensate for her dyslexia. Taussig found her way to cardiology despite being edged out of programs at three—*three*—universities: Harvard, Boston, and Johns Hopkins. At Harvard, the rejection was particularly harsh. Because of her gender, Taussig wasn't allowed in Harvard's medical school, so she inquired about its newly opened School of Public Health, which overlapped with medicine and did admit women. The answer surprised her: women could attend, sure, but their efforts wouldn't earn them a degree. "Who is going to be such a fool as to spend four years studying and not get a degree?" Taussig asked. The dean replied coolly, "No one, I hope." She did not enter the program.

It was in this way that Taussig ping-ponged from medical school to public health to cardiac research to pediatrics to pediatric cardiology. Looking back, she saw the places that rejected her as a route to greater opportunity. In 1930, she finally found her place as the director of pediatric cardiology at the Johns Hopkins children's heart clinic (now called the Helen B. Taussig Congenital Heart Center). At first it was a lean operation. Taussig got assistance from a social worker and a technician, who jumped in to answer phones and file paperwork when needed. In the early days, there was a perception at the hospital that by simply treating patients, Taussig was taking them from medical students, who might learn something from the meeting. So Taussig saw what patients she could and gathered data without a clear idea of how she would eventually use it.

A groundbreaking surgery opened up bright new possibilities for her patients. In 1939, a Harvard surgeon performed a procedure aimed at fixing ductus arteriosus closure. The ductus arteriosus is an opening in the heart that joins two important blood vessels. In the womb, it's supposed to be open, but as a baby's lungs begin to fill with air, the tunnel joining the two arteries should close. If the hole doesn't clamp shut automatically, babies get too much blood to their lungs, which can lead to congestive heart failure and oxygen-poor blood flowing through the body, turning the infants blue. The Harvard surgeon developed a procedure to close the hole manually.

By this point, Taussig had been hard at work for almost a decade. She saw ductus arteriosus patients, but she also saw patients with multiple heart abnormalities who seemed to benefit from an open ductus. In some cases, the opening indirectly shuttled enough blood to the lungs to keep the patient alive. Taussig thought perhaps surgery could open the ductus as well as close it.

Taussig floated her idea to the Harvard surgeon. "Madam," he replied, "I close ductuses. I don't create them." Other surgeons were similarly skeptical, and colleagues expressed annoyance that she wouldn't drop the idea. Finally, after two years of campaigning, Taussig convinced Johns Hopkins's brand-new chief of surgery, Alfred Blalock, to get on board. Blalock asked Vivien Thomas, a technician at the Hopkins research lab, to figure out what surgical steps would be needed to nail the procedure. In 1944, with instruction from Thomas, Blalock performed the first successful Blalock-Taussig shunt on a fifteen-month-old girl. For the third patient, the surgery caused an immediate change in the child's appearance. Taussig remembered the moment fondly, saying, "I suppose nothing would ever give me as much delight as seeing the first patient change from blue to pink in the operating room . . . bright pink cheeks and bright lips. Oh, what a lovely color."

So began a whole new era of pediatric cardiology. All of a sudden, physicians rushed to Taussig's quiet specialty. She remembered it like this: "Dr. Gross [of Harvard] unlocked the gate . . . I opened it; Dr. Blalock and I galloped in, quickly followed by a stream of patients, surgeons, cardiologists, and pediatricians." In 1947, as a culmination of twenty years of research, Taussig literally wrote the textbook on congenital heart defects.

Taussig felt strongly that the new droves of pediatric cardiologists shouldn't have to cobble together an education as haphazardly as she'd had to. With funding from the National Institutes of Health and the US Children's Bureau, pediatric cardiology got an official training program at Johns Hopkins, with Taussig at the helm. Over the years, Taussig taught some 130 young doctors how to succeed in the field she'd started. She emphasized that patient care was an essential component of clinical training: she insisted that physicians treat children as children and not like sick kids, and she believed that compassion and patience were essential in dealing with both the patients and their stressed-out families. Her students, so taken with her verve for the human heart, proudly called themselves "the knights of Taussig."

By the time she died in 1986, she had published forty papers postretirement, served as the American Heart Association's first female president, and received the Presidential Medal of Freedom, given to her by President Lyndon B. Johnson. Taussig was also instrumental in convincing the US Food and Drug Administration to block a medicine that she believed (rightly) caused birth defects.

Over the course of her career, Taussig did an extraordinary amount for the heart. But she never forgot what it felt like to have her hands on it. "You have your sadnesses as well as your successes," Taussig admitted. "One reads all about the successful operation, but not about the unsuccessful ones, the sorrow and background of hard work. On the whole, though, I think I've done more good than harm."

ELSIE WIDDOWSON
1906–2000
Nutrition · British

With a pillow on her lap and a syringe in her left hand, Elsie Widdowson injected a mixture of iron, calcium, and magnesium into her right arm. Going into the experiment, Widdowson and her research partner, Robert McCance, assumed that our bodies excrete iron; however, based on their experiments in 1934, they realized that our bodies actually absorb it.

When Widdowson began studying nutrition in 1933, it was still an emerging field called dietetics. She entered into the discipline on the recommendation of an adviser, several years after earning her PhD. Previously, Widdowson had taken a position in the plant physiology department at Imperial College London, where she monitored changes in apple carbohydrates. The job required twice-monthly apple-picking field trips to Kent, a county southeast of London, so Widdowson could monitor the fruit's composition at different stages in its life cycle, from its first blossom to storage.

After the study was over, she dabbled in biochemistry at Middlesex Hospital's Courtauld Institute. Widdowson didn't dislike apples, but she hoped to get closer to research that would more directly benefit humans. She took a position at King's College Hospital in London in 1933.

Before Widdowson met McCance officially, she was aware of him. He was the scientist cooking up slabs of meat to learn about their chemical composition. The two scientists had fruit research in common. When the pair finally got to talking, Widdowson informed McCance that he'd made a significant error in one of his assessments. Because he had failed to take into account a change in fructose, his carbohydrate numbers were too low; his study was wrong. McCance suggested they join forces. They would remain research partners until McCance's death in 1993.

By the time they started working together, McCance was already well on his way to having a few major food groups analyzed; he'd nearly knocked out the nutrition information for meat, fish, fruits, and vegetables. On an outing with her family in 1934, an idea suddenly struck Widdowson. Those initial categories were important, but why not go all in? Widdowson believed they should analyze everything—sweets, dairy, cereals, beverages—*everything*.

The Chemical Composition of Foods was published in 1940. With fifteen thousand values, it was the first comprehensive compendium of nutrition information for cooked and raw foods ever published.

Meanwhile, Widdowson and McCance maintained a steady stream of side projects. In nutrition research in the mid-1930s, there was still much that researchers didn't know. In one study, Widdowson and McCance wanted to learn about how salt deficiency affects the body. They rounded up some healthy (but reluctant) subjects and put them on a salt-free diet for two weeks. Each participant agreed to spend two hours per day in a podlike warming contraption that forced perspiration. With a long lab coat and her trademark braids, worn Princess Leia style, Widdowson hosed down subjects and their plastic pod sheet after the sessions. The researchers analyzed the runoff for salt content. When sufficiently salt-depleted, the weakened participants were subjected to an array of tests, including ones looking at kidney function.

Widdowson and McCance were the first to show just how important fluid and salt are for the body to work properly. Today, hospitals keep a close watch over these levels, especially in the case of kidney disease, heart attack, or diabetes.

Much of Widdowson's work during the 1940s responded to the urgent nutritional needs of populations as a result of World War II. It was during this time that Widdowson and McCance earned their titles as creators of "the modern loaf," a loaf of bread enriched with calcium. With meat, sugar, and dairy in limited supply, the British government was concerned about having enough nutritious food for its citizens. Widdowson and McCance predicted that their compatriots would do just fine eating a diet composed of cabbage, potatoes, and bread—a few food staples in abundant supply. To test the veracity of their hypothesis, for three months Widdowson and her colleagues all gave the simple, color-free diet a try. The study ended with a rigorous two-week hike-a-thon in England's Lake District.

McCance rode his bike there—a two-plus-day trip—and Widdowson drove up with other colleagues. The group hiked every day and took notes on how the expeditions went. On one of the days, McCance traversed thirty-six miles, powered mainly by cabbage, potatoes, and bread. Based on their experiments, the simple diet was deemed a grand success. Its one main drawback was that it was missing a bit of calcium. Calcium helps our teeth and bones stay healthy, our blood to clot, and our heartbeat remain normal. The researchers added calcium into the diet by supplementing flour with chalk. When rationing went into effect during World War II, the British government gave their pared-down diet a big public relations push. The government suggested that families keep these foods handy to stay healthy. Although food was scarce, at no other time in English history had the population eaten healthier.

After the war ended, Widdowson traveled to Germany to help find solutions for the malnourished. Bread, again, was of particular interest. Widdowson went from orphanage to orphanage in the thick of winter to recruit locations for a bread study that would compare different refinement processes. For eighteen months, Widdowson monitored orphaned children's height and weight and matched the results against the type of bread they consumed. The level of enrichment in the bread flour didn't seem to make a difference, but while she was there, Widdowson noticed sizable changes in the children's weight and growth that seemingly had nothing to do with the loaf. At one orphanage, growth slowed dramatically at about the same time the children's weights at the other test site suddenly took off. Concerned as to the cause, Widdowson launched an examination into what external factors might be at play. By process of elimination, Widdowson discovered that the change was due to a particularly cruel housemother who had transferred from the first test location to the second. Where she was present, children stopped growing and gaining weight. Widdowson concluded, "Tender loving care of children and careful handling of animals may make all the difference to the successful outcome of a carefully planned experiment."

Widdowson's hands-on approach to research went awry only a few times. Once, when she and McCance injected themselves with substances in the name of nutrition research, they wound up on the floor, writhing with fever, tremors, and body aches. A colleague took them home to nurse them back to health. Nevertheless, Widdowson and McCance carried on, collecting their samples even through cold sweats. "A slight accident," they conceded.

Widdowson loved really digging into a problem. On some occasions, that meant throwing a dead baby seal in the trunk and driving it from Scotland to Cambridge to analyze its fat content. On others, she ran back and forth through an airport's metal detector to figure out what on earth could be causing all the beeping. The allure of the experiment was just too enticing to resist. Her lifelong curiosity did the body good.

VIRGINIA APGAR
1909–1974
Medicine · American

Whether she was bicycling with a colleague's child, cheering at a baseball game, or taking flying lessons, Virginia Apgar always kept the following things on her person: a penknife, an endotrachial tube, and a laryngoscope, just in case someone needed an emergency tracheotomy—a procedure in which a hole is punched into a person's windpipe to help them breathe when something is blocking oxygen intake. Even when she was off duty, she was on: "Nobody, but nobody, is going to stop breathing on me."

Apgar was one of the earliest medical doctors to take up anesthesiology. Anesthesiologists worked with surgeons to make sure that patients were safely administered treatments to help them with pain during surgery and in other instances, such as childbirth. Apgar was fast talking and fast thinking, an endless spring of energy. Growing up in New Jersey with an amateur inventor and scientist as a father and a mother caring for a chronically ill brother,

Apgar quipped that her family "never sat down." She didn't sit down, either. In college, while earning top marks studying for a zoology degree, Apgar churned out articles for her college newspaper, became a member of seven sports teams, acted in theater productions, and played violin in the orchestra. After the stock market crash of 1929 hit her family hard, Apgar picked up a collection of odd jobs, including one catching stray cats for the zoology lab. About her constant activity, the editor of her high school yearbook asked, "Frankly, how does she do it?" It was a question that could be applied to any stretch of her very full life.

There were some things she didn't make time for. Apgar had no patience for bureaucracy and red tape, which she'd walk over if she felt they were stopping her from helping a patient or doing the right thing. If an elevator frightened a child, she'd scoop him or her up in her arms and take the stairs. During her medical school residency, Apgar worried that she might have made a mistake that contributed to a patient's decline. She asked for an autopsy, but it wasn't granted. Uncovering the truth became an irrepressible need, so she snuck in and reopened the incision herself. Apgar immediately reported her error to her superior.

She had no tolerance for insincerity or deception, either. Apgar openly admitted her failures and adapted as the field of anesthesiology changed, even when those changes challenged widely accepted beliefs. In fact, Apgar so embraced advancement that her curiosity and openness were instrumental in helping the discipline move forward. It was her flexibility that got her to anesthesiology in the first place.

When Apgar began her internship in surgery at Columbia University in 1933, she was one of only a few women
in the country studying it. She worked under the chair
of surgery, who recommended she shift focus and join
the emerging field of anesthesiology, which, at that point,
wasn't even considered a medical specialty. For her adviser, the recommendation was self-serving. He admired
her abilities and he spotted a need. At the time, if a patient required anesthesia, a nurse stepped in. But as surgeries became more complicated, Apgar's adviser realized
that anesthesia needed to keep pace. He required highly
skilled practitioners talented and driven enough to forge
the way in a rapidly emerging field. Virginia Apgar had
those qualities.

Apgar spent a year away from Columbia to train. When
she returned in 1937, she laid out a plan for how the division of anesthesia would function within the Department of Surgery at Presbyterian Hospital. She asked for a
title (director), suggested an organizational structure, and
mapped out how to establish residencies and bring in more
specialists without displacing the nurses already working
in anesthesiology. For eleven years, Apgar headed the division, training medical students, recruiting residents, and
doing research. She played a major part in helping the specialty grow, but when the division became a department, a
male colleague was given the position of chair.

Apgar turned her focus to babies. While administering
gas to women in labor to help with the pain, she noticed a
curious lack of data. What statistics she did have were puz-
zling. Thanks to deliveries in hospitals instead of at home,
more mothers and babies were living through birth. But

for newborns, the first twenty-four hours remained particularly perilous.

When Apgar looked into the issue, she saw something striking: infants weren't being examined right after birth. Without an immediate appraisal, doctors were missing signs that a baby was, say, starved for oxygen, a factor in half of newborn deaths. Furthermore, Apgar realized that newborns weren't compared against a set of well-being standards. If a mother was given drugs during labor, sometimes her baby would take one breath and not take another for several minutes. Did that count as breathing or not breathing? The answer depended on the delivering physician. Apgar stated what now sounds obvious: a baby shows clear signs when it's struggling, and all babies should be monitored for these signs.

Apgar was vocal about the need for better assessments for newborns. One medical resident asked, how would one go about doing a quick, standardized assessment? "That's easy," she replied, grabbing a nearby piece of paper. "You would do it like this."

The scoring system she outlined covered five major areas requiring a physician's attention: heart rate, respiration, reflex irritability, muscle tone, and color. Each was rated on a scale of 0 to 2. Almost immediately, Apgar and some colleagues tested the system and found connections between scores and a baby's health. Low scores indicated carbon dioxide and blood pH problems. A baby was almost always in need of resuscitation if it had an overall score of 3 or less.

A single baby's score was powerful, but the effect of analyzing thousands of them was like a field of fallen autumn leaves suddenly sorted into colors. All these little bits of evidence started to show patterns. Lower scores correlated with certain methods of delivery and types of anesthesia given to the mother. Before Apgar's efficient scoring system, doctors just didn't see these connections—or didn't have data consistent enough to prove them. The scoring system became a foundation for better public health statistical models. It spread from New York to hospitals across the country.

When it reached Denver, the score finally got its famous name. In 1961, nine years after its initial presentation, a medical resident came up with a catchy mnemonic device:

A: Appearance (Color)
P: Pulse (Heart rate)
G: Grimace (Reflex irritability)
A: Activity (Muscle tone)
R: Respiration

And there it was, the Apgar score. Apgar (the anesthesiologist) loved it.

Meanwhile, Apgar didn't feel adequately equipped to deal with the data pouring in. Always open to things that would make her a better doctor, Apgar took a break from her duties at the hospital to pursue a master's degree in public health. Spotting an opportunity, the National Foundation for Infantile Paralysis, later the March of Dimes, swooped in and made her an offer.

Here, as ever, her curiosity drove her decision making. Enticed by the idea of a midlife career change, Apgar finished her degree and leapt into her new role as chief of the organization's new Division of Congenital Malformations.

For fourteen years, Apgar flew across the country, spreading information on the reproductive process and trying to dispel the stigma associated with congenital birth defects. Her quick and witty personality made her a favorite of TV hosts and the patients she visited. As it was often said, she was a "people doctor," as quick to connect with patients as with viewers and absolutely everyone else she met. "Her warmth and interest give you the feeling that her arms are around you, even though she never touches you," said one volunteer who worked with her. With Apgar in a leading role, the foundation doubled its income.

Apgar worked with people, flew planes, and cheered for baseball games (her colleagues and friends panting behind her) until her own health got in the way. Although she died in 1974, her score is still around. For the better part of the last century, it has protected babies all over the world.

JANE WRIGHT

1919–2013
Medicine · American

For her pioneering work in cancer treatment, Jane Wright was known as "the mother of chemotherapy."

But she was nearly known by another name. When Wright first started at Smith College in Northampton, Massachusetts, she wanted to be a "renowned artist." On the advice of her father, she switched from painting to premed. Wright came from a long line of high-profile doctors. Her grandfathers, Ceah Ketcham Wright and William Fletcher Penn, were both physicians. The latter was the first African American to graduate from Yale's medical school. Wright's father, Louis Tompkins Wright, was a highly respected surgeon and cancer researcher. Perhaps, her father suggested, she should major in something with a more secure route to employment. She rose to the challenge.

Wright entered premed extremely determined, not only to do well in her classes but also to keep up with everything else she enjoyed. Wright balanced her medical school responsibilities with swim team practices and editing the yearbook. She graduated from Smith in 1942 and went on to receive an MD from New York Medical College in 1945. She was a bottomless well of energy. Her supervisor at Bellevue Hospital called her the most promising intern to have worked with him. She may have been a talented artist, but Wright was quickly proving herself an excellent doctor, too.

As she trained, her father's stellar reputation in the medical community set a constant example for her own studies. That is to say, like a friend always jogging fifteen feet ahead, the accomplishments of Louis Tompkins Wright could be both motivating and tiresome. "His being so good really makes it very difficult," Wright admitted in an interview following her graduation from medical school. "You feel you have to do better. Everyone knows who Papa is."

Seeing her promise, in 1949, Louis invited his daughter to come work with him at Harlem Hospital's Cancer Research Foundation, an organization he'd recently founded. Together they dove into what Wright called "the Cinderella" of cancer research: chemotherapy.

When Wright and her father started working together, physicians and scientists were just—*just*—starting to find treatments that could affect spreading cancer cells. In 1945, the director of cancer research at Columbia University described the scope of the task: "It is almost, not quite, but almost as hard as finding some agent that will dissolve away the left ear, say, yet leave the right ear unharmed—so slight is the difference between the cancer cell and its normal ancestor."

Scientists had made some headway with a chemical

related to mustard gas, called nitrogen mustard. Using a chemical weapon to treat cancer wasn't an obvious choice. But an unrelated tragedy—a navy ship that sank in 1943 while carrying mustard gas—gave scientists a tip that something in the chemical might work for cancer patients. When the ship went down, the mustard gas leaked. Many of the soldiers exposed died. During the gassed soldiers' autopsies, it was discovered that the chemical annihilated white blood cells—the ones that protect the body against infection. White blood cells are also the ones that grow cancer in leukemia patients. In 1946, the first cancer patient injected with nitrogen mustard saw an improvement.

So for three years, until Louis's death in 1952, Wright and her father tested drugs they hoped would force leukemia into remission, trying as it were to differentiate the left ear from the right. When her father passed away, Wright stepped up as the head of the research group he had founded. She was just thirty-three.

"Lollygagging," says Wright's daughter, was just not in her nature. Weekday or weekend, at home or on vacation, on her way to the lab, in a restaurant, or boating in Michigan, Wright was up early and dressed to the nines. She shot up through the ranks of Harlem Hospital and then to the top of New York Medical College. By 1967, there was not another African American woman in a nationally recognized medical institution with a more prestigious position.

Over the course of her career, Wright steadily advanced the effectiveness of cancer therapies. One of her most important insights was that one magical solution wasn't going to swoop in and cure cancer for everybody. Say researchers find a really good group of drugs to beat back breast cancer. When that therapy is applied to a different type of cancer—perhaps lung or colon—it might flop. Not even two cases of the same type of cancer can reliably be treated identically. If cancer cells spread quickly and the treatment is off, patients lose crucial time to dead-end therapies.

For twenty-two years starting in 1953, Wright worked on made-to-order solutions. When someone came in sick, Wright took a sample from the patient's tumor so she could grow those cancer cells in a lab. She used the sample—not the patient—to test drive a drug's ability to vanquish the disease. An effective drug mixture in the lab meant it was worth advancing the therapy to the body. The approach didn't waste a patient's time on ineffective drugs, and it was faster and more personalized than using mice as proxies.

Wright also broke new ground on drug delivery. When cancer showed up in hard-to-reach places like the kidneys, surgery was often the default method of tumor extraction. Wright developed a system that would funnel drugs to a targeted area via catheter.

Wright was extremely determined but always modest. Many of her accomplishments were unknown to her own daughters until her death, when friends and colleagues spoke about them publicly. Her daughter Alison felt one comment was particularly fitting of her mother. "She was one of the few people that actually got to do what she wanted to do with her life."

FLORENCE NIGHTINGALE

1820–1910
Statistics · British

Florence Nightingale's name is synonymous with nursing. She's the "lady with the lamp," the compassionate caretaker who checked in on ailing soldiers in the middle of the night. She recognized how atrocious the conditions were in wartime hospitals and lobbied for better standards, based on the needs of patients. It was important work—the foundation of modern nursing—but her statistical analysis of big public health problems is arguably just as influential. In fact, the principles she developed while designing data-gathering tools, and the methods of data analysis and preparation she hammered out, marked the beginning of evidence-based medicine.

On a color-coded page labeled *Diagrams,* Florence Nightingale drew a delicate circular chart. Divided in two different ways, the chart looked like a darts target, a series of concentric circles sliced into pie-like wedges. The wedges were labeled like a clock, but with months replacing the numbers, starting with July at the top, August at 1, September at 2, and so on. Each ring represented a number. The smallest ring—the one in the center—was labeled 100; the second, 200; the outermost circle, 300.

There was a shaded portion of the chart that indicated the number of deaths in British Army hospitals per month from April 1854 to March 1855, during the Crimean War. In July, the light green area (infectious diseases) topped out just above 150. As it got colder, the death toll rose, and a spotlight of green splashed down the page, traveling far beyond the last ring. The number of people who died from wounds was fewer than 50. The number of deaths by diseases in the same month: 1,023.

When Nightingale was sent to Turkey to support military hospitals, details about the deplorable conditions had already made their way to the newspapers. Illness was taking down soldiers faster than enemy bullets. Nightingale quantified those sensational stories. The charts she created—what she called coxcombs, now known as polar-area diagrams—were so striking in their visual assessment that when Nightingale began lobbying for changes that would improve soldiers' health, she had a sturdy platform to stand on. In 1856, Nightingale took her concerns to Queen Victoria and Prince Albert.

It took the British secretary of state for war less than a year from Nightingale's return from Crimea to issue an order that called for the creation of a statistical branch of the Army Medical Department. Nightingale's data and her visualizations provided rapid clarity about the failings of military hospitals; improper sanitation was to blame.

After offering her diagnosis, Nightingale laid out a clear set of standards aimed at improving conditions for patients in hospitals. Some recommendations, like installing easy-to-clean walls, floors, and equipment or offering patients food with nutritional value, now seem basic. But ideal qualities like access to light and quiet are ones that hospitals still strive for today.

In her book *Notes on Nursing,* Nightingale's best-known offering, she explained that "the symptoms or the sufferings generally considered to be inevitable or incident to the disease are very often not symptoms of the disease at all, but of something quite different—of the want of fresh air, or of light, or of warmth, or of quiet, or of cleanliness, or of punctuality and care in the administration of diet." Bedsores, for instance, were something that nurses had direct control over. And transferring those burdens from patient to caretaker marked a seismic shift in philosophy.

Through observation and statistical analysis of census data, Nightingale designed a curriculum for nurses. It provided them with adequate training for the very first time. The program had its grand unveiling in 1860 at a brand-new school, the Nightingale School of Nursing at St. Thomas' Hospital in London, funded through private donations. Feeling ill, Nightingale wasn't able to attend the opening ceremony.

As Nightingale fought to improve the health of others, she spent more and more time at home trying to keep herself well. For decades, she was plagued with an illness historians now think was brucellosis—a disease that can cause pain, headaches, fever, and other symptoms that might not go away for years. During the time of her illness, she retreated to her room and rarely left.

Although poor health eventually stopped Nightingale from making public appearances, it didn't stop her from working. She dove into statistics, which gave her a reliable way to identify what patients needed to be healthier. The better the information, the more effectively Nightingale could go about initiating change. Nightingale also kept up a lively correspondence in letters. By the end of her life, she was writing letters twelve hours a day, the method she'd long used for keeping up with statisticians, friends, and her efforts to update nursing practices she led in India and Australia. If she received an inquiry about the proper material for hospital walls, Nightingale would whip out thirteen pages on the intricacies of a certain kind of cement. Because letter writing was her primary mode of communication, Nightingale became highly skilled in the art, always present, attentive, and sensitive to her audience.

Becoming a global icon during her lifetime made Nightingale deeply uncomfortable. The focus, she thought, should be on the patient. Though she had long before hung up her lamp, it continued to shine on her, and deservedly so.

BIOLOGY

Rachel Carson published her book *Silent Spring* in 1951. The book's vivid descriptions of pesticides and their damaging effects on wildlife and the environment changed the way the United States viewed environmental protection forever. Her book spurred the birth of the Environmental Protection Agency, Earth Day, and new regulations that monitor pesticide use and other activities that might harm animals, air, water, or land, and in turn, people. It didn't just make a splash; it created a tidal wave.

The breakthroughs by women in this section activated entirely new areas of research. Jeanne Villepreux-Power's invention of the aquarium in 1832 allowed scientists to examine sea creatures in a lab—and paved the way for those massive glass aquariums that hold jellyfish and octopus and spotted dragonet. Barbara McClintock and Rosalind Franklin opened up our understanding of DNA, giving us more clarity on how the building blocks fit together to make us who we are. And Mary Anning discovered a dinosaur before her thirteenth birthday, continuing on to be a force in prehistoric fossil discovery, even though she didn't get nearly as much credit as she deserved. Anning didn't require permission to discover fossils. She went out to the sea-lined cliffs regularly because she loved hunting for buried treasures.

Maria Sibylla Merian was born in 1647; of all the people in this book, she's born the earliest. Her specialty? Bugs. Even though it would be centuries until women would gain a foothold in the sciences, biology offered a way in. Merian found her six-legged research subjects everywhere she went. Her illustrated observations of a caterpillar's metamorphosis into a butterfly gave naturalists a new perspective on the process.

In Italy in 1940, Rita Levi-Montalcini was barred from practicing medicine or research during World War II because she was Jewish. However, she was able to carry out experiments in a secret bedroom lab, using chicken eggs donated by a neighbor. The quest for a better understanding of the world was self-driven. Levi-Montalcini and the others in this section breezed right past those who told them no, and chased after their passions by using what was around them. Stomping through lakes, sifting through silt, gathering creepy-crawlies, and slicing through chicken eggs is important work—and thrilling. They understood that gaining access to biological sciences is as easy as observing the world around you.

MARIA SIBYLLA MERIAN

1647–1717

Entomology · German

Maria Sibylla Merian loved bugs long before scientists had uncovered their mysteries, and she loved them at a time when few people were interested in those vile, disgusting creatures. Acquaintances assigned credit or blame to her mother, who had looked at a collection of insects while Merian was still in the womb. They believed something about those pinned and polished bodies, shimmering powdery wings, and articulated legs instilled a fascination in the child growing inside her.

As a youngster, Merian kept a record of her beloved creatures (and their favorite hideouts) by learning how to draw them. Merian's stepfather was a painter and art dealer, and it was from him that she learned how to mix pigments for watercolors by working the fine grains with a mortar and pestle, dropping the powder into water, and then sealing the solution with acacia tree sap, which helped the color bind to the page. To understand anatomical forms,

Merian traced existing work. She followed the powerful zigzags of a grasshopper's leg and the creases of a snail shell as it spiraled outward.

At age thirteen, Merian started bringing her bugs into her home. She nurtured a little colony of silkworms, feeding them mulberry leaves or scraps of lettuce in a pinch. Merian took notes and painted the specimens as they mowed through their food, spun themselves into a "date pit" (a German expression for a cocoon), and burst open. She waited with giddy anticipation to see what would emerge. A wet moth? A cloud of flies? Nothing at all? Merian painted every stage and variation.

Naturalists weren't paying much attention to insects during the time Merian studied them. Even the bugs' ability to reproduce was largely a mystery. When flies sprouted from rotten meat or dung, many believed they had spontaneously generated. There were even recipes that explained how, with a few simple ingredients, one could grow creatures like bees and scorpions. Want a worm? Mix one part dead flies and one part honey water on a copper plate. Warm the plate with smoldering ashes until . . . Voilà! Worms appeared.

A well-known naturalist claimed that butterflies actually lived within caterpillar bodies—and that he could do a fancy trick with boiling water, vinegar, and wine to prove it. When previous illustrators drew the stages of a silkworm's metamorphosis, each form was filed separately, worms next to other worms and butterflies with butterflies. Its life cycle was broken up into categories; the arc of the caterpillar's life was hidden.

Merian saw each stage in a bug's life cycle as a continuous process, when few other naturalists were making connections between the worm and the butterfly. In her illustrations, she put her specimens into their environments, capturing them crawling on leaves with curling seams, flying over flowers' stretching tendrils, or circling around stems, at a time when most illustrators worked from display cases.

In 1679, Merian published her first major work on insects, a two-volume book of entomological illustrations focused on metamorphosis. With notes on food preferences and the bugs' activities logged next to each image, Merian placed herself firmly within the tradition of naturalist observation.

As her career evolved, so did her personal life. In rapid succession, Merian split from her husband and moved from her native Germany to Holland with her mother and two daughters to join a religious sect. The group wasn't big into personal possessions, so for a while Merian stopped her illustrations.

By 1691, the sect was flailing. It struggled to keep its European members healthy and support expeditions to Suriname, a Dutch colony in South America, where the group hoped to set up a homestead. In one embarrassing incident, pirates robbed and stripped naked one of the sect's convoys, leaving them to arrive unclothed.

When the sect in Holland dissolved, Merian and her daughters relocated to Amsterdam. As hope for a new religious community abroad faded, Merian felt her own personal interest in Suriname swell. Over the years, she'd collected bugs on bridges, in backyards, in rural fields, and in meticulously manicured gardens. Friends boxed up their exotic finds and shipped them over for her to observe. After a lifetime studying the same specimens, Merian desperately wanted to go someplace where she could discover more.

In 1699, at age fifty-two, Merian and her youngest daughter loaded up their art supplies and hopped on a ship for Suriname, financed by years of commissions and the sale of 255 paintings. The goal was to devote five years to exploring and illustrating the insects abroad.

In Suriname, a whole world of new specimens kept her plenty busy—and occasionally at risk. She braved the appealing fuzz of a red-and-white caterpillar, its poisonous barbs disguised in bright colors. But for Merian, the danger made the discovery even more interesting. She wrapped up the caterpillar and carried it home. Eventually, she moved her expeditions farther afield, and when she finally felt comfortable enough to go out into the rain forest, Merian followed a path forged by slaves, a fresh-cut path made specifically for specimen collecting.

The bugs brought Merian to Suriname, but they also sent her home. Forced back to Europe three years early by malaria and the heat, Merian was still able to whip her two years abroad into her life's greatest work. *The Metamorphosis of the Insects of Suriname* was published in 1705, when she was fifty-eight. The book included sixty engravings that illustrated a creature's entire life cycle—just as she had done in her youth—with notes about its habits and environment. The vivid, writhing animals nearly crawled off the page.

The book brought Merian to a final transformation. One of the very first entomologists, Merian broke new ground in observing and documenting the stages of metamorphosis. By treating the insect life cycle as something worthy of rigorous study, she ushered in a new wave of scientists who followed her lead. Thirty years after *Insects of Suriname* was published, a French biologist developed the first classification system for bugs. Merian set the stage for one of the most significant moments in entomological history.

JEANNE VILLEPREUX-POWER

1794–1871
Biology · French

Jeanne Villepreux-Power spent a decade observing the ocean's creatures before her work was swallowed by it. Villepreux-Power wasn't on the ship when it sank, but years of her scientific research plunged into the depths. The loss was substantial, but if anyone was capable of bobbing above the water, it was Villepreux-Power. By this point in her life, she had already reinvented herself twice.

Growing up a shoemaker's daughter in tiny Juillac, France, Jeanne Villepreux belonged in a larger arena. At eighteen, she left her hometown for a place grand enough to match her abilities and interests: Paris. Some say she walked there; others say she found a ride. Either way, the journey was fueled by determination.

In Paris, Villepreux landed a position as an assistant to a dressmaker, where she watched, worked, and experimented. In a few years, she was able to prove her own considerable talents. In 1816, when Princess Caroline, the daughter of the king of the Two Sicilies, married Charles-

Ferdinand de Bourbon, the nephew of King Louis XVIII, she was wearing a dress designed by Villepreux. The garment captivated Europe's upper ranks, and Villepreux—still in her early twenties—found herself courted not only for her clothes but also for her hand in marriage.

Two years later, Villepreux married the English merchant James Power, based in Messina, Sicily. As she began her life on the island, Villepreux-Power realized the location offered her another opportunity for reinvention. Sicily was rich with varieties of flora and fauna unfamiliar to her. To learn more about her adopted environment, Villepreux-Power embarked on a project to take inventory of the island's ecosystem while teaching herself natural history. The goal was to catalog the plants, animals, and ocean life surrounding her waterfront abode.

In 1832, Villepreux-Power began studying a tiny relative of the octopus, called the paper nautilus. Its shell, which the nautilus uses to navigate the ocean waters, had been a mystery to scientists dating as far back as 300 BC, when Aristotle hypothesized that the creatures used their tentacles as both oars and sails to steer their brittle vessel like a boat. For centuries, the shell's utility and its origin remained unknown, but in the nineteenth century, the prevailing thinking was that the shell was an acquired home, like the ones hermit crabs procure. Villepreux-Power wasn't so sure.

Now, there was only so much one could learn by plucking a creature from its briny environment to study it. So in 1832, Villepreux-Power invented a container to aid her observations. It worked by keeping aquatic creatures alive in their own ecosystem—even while extracted from the ocean. She designed a glass case, and that case became the first recognizable aquarium. With it, Villepreux-Power was able to watch her subjects long enough to discover that the shy paper nautilus doesn't scavenge her chambered shell at all; she *produces* it herself.

For the scientific community, both the stage Villepreux-Power designed for her experiments and the results gathered within it were big revelations. In 1858, the British paleontologist Richard Owen (the man responsible for coining the word *dinosaur*) anointed Villepreux-Power the mother of *aquariophily*. The Zoological Society of London named the glass boxes "power cages" after their multitalented inventor.

Eleven years after designing her first "power cage," Villepreux-Power continued to experiment with boxes she dipped in the sea. During that time, she added wooden structures and anchors to a submersible model so that it could plunge deeper into the ocean. In her cages, Villepreux-Power watched starfish act out their private rituals of meal preparation and assessed the stomach content of mollusks.

Over her lifetime, Villepreux-Power gained membership in more than a dozen scientific academies throughout Europe—the Zoological Society of London and the Gioenian Academy of Natural Sciences in Catania, Italy, among them. After her death in 1871, the *North American Review* called her "one of the most eminent naturalists of the century," and called the aquarium an "incalculable" contribution to marine zoology. In 1997, Villepreux-Power ascended even higher when a large crater on Venus was named in her honor.

MARY ANNING

1799–1847
Paleontology · British

Before she was struck by lightning, Mary Anning was a dull child. But after she was lifted from the grisly scene and sponged off (her babysitter and two friends dead and a horse-riding event halted), the baby had changed. The once-placid infant had been zapped into a new state, forever after described as "lively and intelligent."

In a life filled with difficulties, electrocution was a rare (if bizarre) stroke of luck. Anning's family was poor. Of ten children, she and her brother were the only two who survived into adulthood. Her father was a carpenter who supplemented his meager income by hawking seaside souvenirs to tourists. The most sought-after trinket: fossils.

Anning's father pulled his specimens from limestone and shale cliffs of Lyme Regis, England. That ragged edge of their hometown ran along the sea. When a storm thundered in, large sheets of rock would tumble into the water, exposing sections of the area's history. Swooping in at just

the right moment, Anning's father would find an assort-
ment of shells and bones ripe for the picking.

Anning learned the trade from her father at age ten.
After he died in 1810 from tuberculosis, Anning and her
brother made the trips to the bluffs alone. Their haul was
mostly shells and small fossils in the beginning. But in
1811, Anning's brother Joseph noticed a bone face emerging from the rock. Several weeks later, with a small ham-
mer, Anning carefully cleared the sediment from around
the curvature of the skull. The more work she put in, the
more work there was to be done. The skull led to a spine
and then a rib cage and legs. All in all, Anning traced
around the bones of a beast some seventeen feet long with
massive crocodile-like jaws. Two children discovered the
world's first ichthyosaur fossil.

They sold the ichthyosaur (which means "fish-lizard")
to the lord of a nearby manor for twenty-three British
pounds—several hundred dollars in today's currency. The
ichthyosaur marked Anning's first substantial contribution
to paleontology, but the fish-lizard was only the beginning.

Anning and her brother were not the first people
to discover fossils in Lyme Regis. Locals had picked up
strangely shaped bones here and there. Some believed that
they were God's embellishments, and others thought the
fossilized remnants might have come from the flood that
lifted Noah's ark. Anning's bones, however, told another
story. By excavating fully articulated creatures from Lyme
Regis's unstable rock, she had revealed specimens unlike
anything anyone had ever seen.

With her dog acting as her sidekick after her brother

lost interest, Anning surveyed the cliffs following storms
and landslides, combing through the debris for specimens.
The stones, shells, and bones she retrieved filled up a tiny
roadside shop.

In 1823, Anning discovered a plesiosaur (then referred
to as a sea dragon), and five years later, she delivered a
pterodactylus (called a flying dragon). Anning's ability to
spot specimens, sort them, sketch them, and present them
was unparalleled. She studied up on the ancient reptiles
she found. Anning's moneyed patrons were routinely impressed by her breadth of knowledge.

Scientists profited greatly from her work, but because
of her class and gender, the academic discussions sparked
by her findings always excluded her. When Mary Anning's
discoveries appeared in journals, her name was edited out.
Anning's patrons arranged for a small stipend to fund her
collecting, but the real profit—scientific acclaim—went to
others.

Anning's accomplishments weren't respected in Lyme
Regis, either; neighbors considered her nothing more than
a tourist attraction. To a young correspondent in London,
Anning wrote, "I beg your pardon for distrusting your
friendship. The world has used me so unkindly, I fear it
has made me suspicious of everyone." She spent her life
poor and largely alone. Her dog, Tray, was killed in a land-
slide.

The record of Anning's contributions has always tee-
tered dangerously close to being covered over. In 1859,
twelve years after Anning's death from breast cancer at
age forty-seven, Charles Darwin published *On the Origin*

of Species. The work was likely influenced by Anning's prehistoric discoveries. There were a few bright flashes of recognition along the way. In 1865, Charles Dickens wrote an article about Anning's life in *All the Year Round,* a journal he edited. It concluded with the line, "The carpenter's daughter has won a name for herself, and has deserved to win it."

BARBARA McCLINTOCK

1902–1992
Genetics · American

Freedom and independence felt like home to McClintock. When she was a baby, her mother used to set her on a pillow and leave her to amuse herself. Simply mulling over the world and all of its amazing patterns and peculiarities was a happy pastime of McClintock's earliest years. "I didn't belong to that family, but I'm glad I was in it," she said. "I was an odd member."

Her outsider status was not so different in the scientific community. Though she absolutely belonged there and was fully absorbed in her work, McClintock never completely integrated. One part of the issue was societal. Getting a faculty position at a university was exponentially harder for women in the 1920s than it was during World War II, when positions opened up for women after men were called to war. Though up to 40 percent of graduate students in the 1920s in the United States were women, that didn't translate into jobs—especially in science. Fewer than 5 percent of female scientists in America were able to land jobs at coed institutions. And even then, the home economics and physical education departments were the biggest hirers. Women rarely rose to posts as prestigious as professor. In the Venn diagram of female biologists hired as professors at major research institutions, the middle was a lonely place. McClintock never got there.

McClintock's work also kept her out of the mainstream. She was either ahead of her time, with experimental methods so dense and complicated that they were difficult for her peers to understand, or she chose subjects that operated outside trends in biology.

During her first year of graduate school at Cornell University, for example, McClintock took it upon herself to identify discrete parts of corn's chromosomes. Chromosomes live in the nucleus of a cell and contain an organism's DNA—the stuff that makes us uniquely who we are. Her short-term adviser, a cryptologist, had been trying to do the same thing for a long time. McClintock saddled up to the microscope and—bam—"I had it done within two or three days—the whole thing done, clear, sharp, nice." She revealed the answer so quickly that it bruised her adviser's ego. McClintock was so thoroughly hopped up on the quest that she hadn't even considered the possibility that she would upstage her superior.

In other instances, her groundbreaking experiments required an interpreter who could explain them. When she laid out her case for the location of genes on corn's distinguishable ten chromosomes, her method remained a mystery to her colleagues until a scientist from another school visited and unpacked the study design for public consumption. "It was so . . . obvious," said the interpreter, "she was something special."

McClintock adored biology at Cornell. She was no typical high achiever, either. Following the acknowledgment of her corn chromosome discovery as a master's student, she attracted a pack of professors and PhDs who trailed her around campus like puppies tumbling after castoff treats, "lapping up the stimulation she provided," said one. Together the group, with McClintock as its intellectual leader, ushered in an especially bright period of genetics—the study of how characteristics are passed from one generation to the next. McClintock proudly recounted how the "very powerful work with chromosomes . . . began to put cytogenetics, working with chromosomes, on the map. . . . The older people couldn't join; they just didn't understand. The young people were the ones who really got the subject going."

After getting her PhD, McClintock spent a few more years at Cornell, publishing papers, teaching botany, and advising students. In 1929, she and a graduate student bred one type of corn having waxy, purple kernels together with another type of corn whose kernels were neither waxy nor purple. McClintock's experiments showed that some kernels inherited one trait but not the other, for example, brightly colored purple kernels without the waxy texture. When McClintock looked at the corn's chromosomes through a microscope, she found that the chromosomes' appearance was noticeably different. In the cases where kernels had one trait but not the other, parts of a chromosome had traded places.

The discovery was hailed as one of the greatest experiments of modern biology. At just twenty-nine years old,

McClintock had proved herself a powerful force in genetics research—but without a permanent faculty position. The head of the department at Cornell was in favor of bringing her on to become a professor, but the rest of the faculty forbade it. So McClintock left, picking up fellowships here and there, searching for a new place to put down roots.

When she was at the University of Missouri, McClintock was known as a troublemaker. The marks against her—wearing pants in the field instead of knickers, allowing students to stay in the lab past their curfew, managing with a firm, no-nonsense style—were practical choices, ones McClintock believed would improve her work and that of others. But to her superiors, her behavior was obstinate. McClintock was excluded from faculty meetings, her requests for research support were denied, and her chances for advancement were made clear: If she ever decided to marry, she'd be fired. If her research partner left the university, she'd be fired. The dean was just waiting for an excuse to let her go.

There are times for perseverance and there are times to get out quick. In 1941, after five years at the University of Missouri, McClintock found the door, slamming it behind her.

Never one to be burdened with possessions (or weighed down by the limited vision of others), McClintock hopped into her Model A Ford and, like a dandelion seed surfing the breeze, set out not knowing where she and her research would land. When she turned her back on the University of Missouri, it was possible she was also losing the career that she'd worked so hard to achieve.

The country's greatest research institutions should have fought over McClintock, but instead, she ended up searching for a space to plant her corn. She found one at Cold Spring Harbor in Long Island, New York. The facility was initially founded in 1890 as a place for high school and college teachers to learn about marine biology. When Mc-Clintock arrived, it was a genetics institute—a workplace for scientists studying how the features of one organism are passed down to the next generation. The atmosphere was ideal for McClintock: she wouldn't have to teach, and there were no restrictions on her research, which would be entirely self-directed. She could wear jeans and stay as late and work as often as she wanted. The place suited her so well that when she socialized, she would invite friends to the lab instead of to her home. Her home was an un-heated, converted garage down the street, used for nothing more than sleep.

McClintock was extraordinarily organized. Clothes in her closet all faced the same direction, and each of her scientific specimens was assiduously labeled. Sometimes she'd get so engrossed in her work that peering into a microscope would feel to her like spelunking through the deep secrets of a cell. "You're not conscious of anything else," she remembered. "You're so absorbed that even small things get big."

At Cold Spring Harbor, McClintock spent six years on her greatest scientific accomplishment. When she finally unveiled her findings to a group of researchers, they re-sponded to her hourlong talk with silence. One listener re-called that the presentation landed "like a lead balloon"—not well at all. McClintock laid out a meticulously researched

case that genetics was much, much more fluid than what
scientists had previously realized, with genes able to switch
on and off and change locations. The prevailing belief was
that genes were like bolted-down pieces of furniture. In
the 1950s, scientists from all different fields of study were
getting into the genetics game; chemists and physicists applied their disciplines to understanding inherited traits.
With so many new ways to look at our genetic makeup,
studying corn—McClintock's preferred research subject—
had fallen out of favor. "I was startled when I found they
didn't understand it, didn't take it seriously," she said of
the talk. "But it didn't bother me. I knew I was right."

McClintock was right. The acceptance of her ideas
didn't come until nearly two decades later, when molecular biologists finally saw in bacteria what McClintock had
seen in corn. At the news, McClintock was overjoyed. "All
the surprises . . . revealed recently give so much fun," she
wrote to a friend. "I am thoroughly enjoying the stimulus
they provide." Public acknowledgment brought a string of
awards—the MacArthur Foundation Fellowship, the Albert Lasker Basic Medical Research Award—but no Nobel
Prize, the greatest award in science. Then finally, in 1983,
thirty-two years after her big but ignored discovery, she
heard her name announced on the radio. Barbara Mc-
Clintock finally won science's most prestigious prize. Her
"discovery of mobile genetic elements" was touted by the
Nobel Committee as "one of the two great discoveries of
our times in genetics."

In the ensuing years, she was asked time and time again
the same question, some delicately worded take on *Were*

you bitter it took so long? Her answer: "No, no, no. You're having a good time. You don't need public recognition, and I mean this quite seriously, you don't need it." With characteristic confidence, she added, "When you know you're right you don't care. It's such a pleasure to carry out an experiment when you think of something. . . . I've had such a good time, I can't imagine having a better one. . . . I've had a very, very satisfying and interesting life."

RACHEL CARSON

1907–1964
Marine Biology · American

Rachel Carson had loved the outdoors ever since she was a child. The birds and plants she observed around her family's rural property and along Pennsylvania's Allegheny River had sparked her imagination for as long as she could remember. Over the years, she found a fossilized fish, hopping birds, and native plants. Inspired by her expeditions, at age eight, Carson wrote a story titled "The Little Brown House" about a pair of wrens looking for shelter. Her well-written tales and her persistence in pitching them enabled Carson to join an underage literary elite of young contributors with published works in the now-defunct children's magazine *St. Nicholas*. (William Faulkner, F. Scott Fitzgerald, e. e. cummings, and E. B. White also published work in the magazine as children.) Carson was fond of noting that she had become a professional writer at age eleven.

When Carson entered the Pennsylvania College for Women on a senatorial district scholarship, earning an

English degree as preparation to become a writer was a natural choice. However, during her undergraduate years, it was biology that she found most thrilling. That fossilized fish? Biology gave her the tools to learn what had happened to it.

After earning a master's degree in zoology, which is the study of animal life, from Johns Hopkins University, Carson found part-time work at the US Bureau of Fisheries. Though she'd chosen science over prose, her former specialty proved useful in her new occupation. Carson's first assignment for the bureau was to write a fifty-two-episode radio program called *Romance Under the Waters*.

"I had given up writing forever, I thought. It never occurred to me that I was merely getting something to write about." Her bosses at the bureau were thrilled with her work; however, the appreciation did not translate monetarily. To supplement her low pay, Carson churned out articles covering conservation issues for the *Baltimore Sun* on a freelance basis.

Although Carson climbed the ranks at the bureau to eventually become an aquatic biologist, her duties never included actual scientific work. Instead, she was asked to do things like edit her colleagues' scientific reports and package a study's results into public brochures.

What she learned at the bureau during the day proved useful to her freelance career in the evenings. In 1937, Carson published a story in the *Atlantic* magazine that examined the sea from the perspective of the animals and plants within it. The article's descriptions of aquatic creatures—and even of their deaths—were mesmerizing. "Every living thing of the ocean, plant and animal alike, returns to the water at the end of its own lifespan the materials that had been temporarily assembled to form its body. So there descends into the depths a gentle, never-ending rain of the disintegrating particles of what once were living creatures of the sunlit surface waters, or of those twilight regions beneath."

Her article led to the publication of her first book, *Under the Sea Wind*. Although it would be Carson's favorite, the volume was a commercial failure, selling only two thousand copies. Carson needed a couple of years to recover from the blow, but both driven and strapped for cash, she pushed forward. Carson wrote another book. When *The Sea Around Us* arrived in 1951, it won the National Book Award for nonfiction and solidified Carson's position as a literary heavyweight. To this day, it's credited as being one of the most successful books ever written about nature.

Carson found the public's interest in nature extremely heartening. "We live in a scientific age; yet we assume that knowledge of science is the prerogative of only a small number of human beings, isolated and priestlike in their laboratories. This is not true," Carson said in a speech. "The materials of science are the materials of life itself. Science is part of the reality of living; it is the what, the how, and the why of everything in our experience."

When we talk about Carson today, we talk about *Silent Spring*. First serialized in the *New Yorker* before being published in book form in 1962, *Silent Spring* chronicled the devastating effects of the overuse of pesticides. The book was startling for its rigorous scientific assessment of how, by spraying for one issue—to get rid of a bug or a weed—without considering how the chemicals would impact everything else, people were often doing more harm than good. It was a beautifully written treatise of horrors aimed at a general audience.

The book's main target was DDT, or dichlorodiphenyltrichloroethane. DDT was the first modern, lab-made insecticide. Credited with curbing malaria and typhus in World War II, DDT was viewed as a panacea—something that fell under the umbrella of, as the DuPont company famously put it, "Better Things for Better Living . . . Through Chemistry." In *Silent Spring,* Carson worried about DDT's rapid and near-universal acceptance. "Almost immediately DDT was hailed as a means of stamping out insect-borne disease and winning the farmers' war against crop destroyers overnight."

So new and revolutionary was the poison and its ability to control pests, Carson argued, that proper precautions in understanding the greater effects of its application were not being taken. Using DDT was like flicking down one domino but ignoring the long line of others tumbling in succession behind it.

Now, Carson believed in science; her entire career was built upon her devotion to it. But by looking at pesticides from only one angle, she argued—as chemical companies were wont to do for their bottom line—they were being irresponsible. Carson laid out her case with scientific studies and observations from the field: twenty-seven species of dead fish in the Colorado River, accidentally poisoned livestock, a greenhouse worker with paralysis.

Silent Spring jump-started the environmental movement and provided the public with a target: the multimillion-dollar chemical industry. In turn, the chemical industry reacted by launching a quarter-million-dollar smear campaign against Carson. She was called hysterical, labeled a spinster, and accused of letting harmless insects terrify her. Whenever Carson or the book set off an outrage, the chemical industry fanned the flames. As a result, in the early 1960s, Carson was at the center of a very public battle between those hoping to preserve nature and those wanting to control it. Fortunately, it was a fight Carson had been preparing for her entire life.

And the people listened. A US Senate subcommittee called Carson in to speak about her research, federal and state organizations started investigating the effects of DDT and other pesticides, and grassroots initiatives began to organize.

Silent Spring was tremendously influential. Three major events in 1970 were inspired by Carson's work. The National Environmental Policy Act promoted "efforts which will prevent or eliminate damage to the environment and biosphere and stimulate the health and welfare of man." A senator from Wisconsin later called it "the most important piece of environmental legislation in our history." In April of that year, the United States had its first Earth Day, and then the Environmental Protection Agency was formed. In a timeline of the EPA's history, *Silent Spring* is the first reference, the official germination of the agency. Carson wouldn't be around to see the changes called for by both the government and individuals as a result of her book. Breast cancer took her too swiftly, just two years after *Silent Spring*'s publication. But her book succeeded in bringing about change. Carson's resounding voice is the foundation of modern environmentalism.

RUTH PATRICK

1907–2013

Biology · American

As a child growing up in Kansas City, Missouri, Ruth Patrick recalled eagerly that she "collected everything: worms,
mushrooms, plants, rocks. I remember the feeling I got
when my father would roll back the top of his big desk in
the library and roll out the microscope. . . . It was miracu-
lous, looking through a window at a whole other world."

She held that interest close as she took the study of
botany from a bachelor's degree earned at Coker College,
in South Carolina, and a PhD earned at the University of
Virginia. Because the Academy of Natural Sciences in Philadelphia had America's best collection of diatoms, Patrick
started working with the institution in graduate school.
She had a long career ahead of her, and when she thought
about those early days, she remembered being "a little
peon." After receiving her PhD in 1934, Patrick stayed on
at the academy as a volunteer curator in the microscopy
department. She took charge of the existing collection of

diatoms, or single-celled algae, and grew it to become one of the most extensive in the world. It wasn't until 1945, though, that the organization came to its senses and started paying Patrick for her work.

Patrick dedicated her life to studying pollution in order to curb it. She took a unique path, choosing to work with big industrial clients like DuPont to lessen their negative environmental impact rather than calling them out. "You can't have society without industry," she told a reporter in 1984. "But on the other hand, industry has to realize that it is a responsible group."

One afternoon in the summer of 1959, while working for DuPont, Ruth Patrick and a colleague were traveling down a river in Ireland when suddenly they found their rowboat close to a British naval vessel. Over the loud-speaker, the bigger ship commanded that the pair "come here at once." Annoyed, Patrick replied, "I will when I finish my business." Patrick was in the middle of impor-tant scientific work. She was watching a cork float down the Lough Foyle. The cork's movements were essential to understanding the river's currents. Stopping would mean losing sight of the cork and the day's work. But the naval vessel insisted. "Come here at once or we'll shoot!"

The navy apparently mistook the cork for a snorkel and the snorkel as a sign of a bigger threat to the ship. After several hours of questioning, Patrick's employer stepped in to explain. Yes, she was measuring the current in prepa-ration for a new DuPont chemical plant to be built in the area. An American ambassador later joked with Patrick at a dinner event, "So you're the lady who was going to blow up the Queen's Navy! That story has gotten all over London!"

Ruth Patrick's influence by that point had nearly spanned the globe. Patrick was the first scientist to show how the health of rivers could be measured by looking at a body of water's tiniest organisms—diatoms. "You see, diatoms are like detectives," she explained. A diatom's cell walls are made of silica, which takes in environmental pollutants. Almost proudly, Patrick told a local PBS affiliate she was able to detect evidence of a nuclear plant disaster that took place in Ukraine by examining diatoms. These simple little organisms could reveal a body of water's history.

And sometimes they did. Patrick's investigation into the Great Salt Lake in the 1930s gave some solid clues about its origin. She found freshwater diatoms layered into the lake's deposits—up to the point when a change occurred. Finding no sand or chlorides, Patrick ruled out a tidal wave as the cause of a sudden shift from fresh water to salt.

Patrick realized that a river's overall biodiversity—the range of plants and animals that call it home—could tell scientists a lot about the body of water's health. Problems with contamination appeared in locations where relatively few organisms lived. If it seems obvious now that thriving communities equal good ecosystems, it's because Patrick pioneered the idea. In 1954, she even invented a device that would take better water samples, called a diatometer.

Diatom sampling satisfied Patrick's adventurous spirit. At age seventy-six, she guessed that she'd waded into some nine hundred rivers, spread out over every continent but

Africa. That same year, she confronted 102-degree temperatures mucking around the Flint River in Georgia. Patrick
continued to pull on her waders to gather river samples
all the way into her nineties. When she couldn't go out
anymore, she moved her work to the lab, coming in every
day to analyze her "lovely" diatoms. A run-in with an ag-
gressive foreign naval operation was just one tiny story in
105 years of scientific adventures.

Patrick influenced the way people thought, not only
about rivers and lakes but also about drinking water,
which she showed was being contaminated regionally by
fertilizer runoff and scptic tank seepage.

Her opinion was sought by a line of presidents. Lyndon B. Johnson asked for her input on water pollution,
and Ronald Reagan consulted her about acid rain. For her
work in industry, at universities, and at the Academy of
Natural Sciences, Bill Clinton awarded Patrick a National
Medal of Science in 1996.

On the eve of Patrick's hundredth birthday, a reporter
brought up a comment from a prominent environmental
scientist regarding her legacy. "I try not to think about it,"
Patrick said. She still had several more years of important
work to do.

RITA LEVI-MONTALCINI

1909–2012
Neuroembryology · Italian

During the last two and a half decades of her 103 years, Italians liked to joke that everyone would recognize the pope, so long as he appeared with Rita Levi-Montalcini. Every Italian knew Rita. Though she stood only five feet three inches tall, the stories of her work and her life were as large and dramatic as her iconic sideswept hair.

There was the time she smuggled a pair of mice on a plane from the United States to Brazil by tucking them away in her purse or pocket—for the sake of her research, of course. Or the years she bicycled door-to-door during World War II, pleading with farmers for donated chicken eggs to feed her "babies." The eggs were actually for her research. Once, Levi-Montalcini talked her way into the copilot seat of an airplane, since that was the only seat open on a fully booked flight. On another flight, when the airline lost her suitcase, and the clothes she had on were wrinkled, she opted to give a lecture in a pressed nightgown rather than appear disheveled in front of an audience.

In life and in her work, Levi-Montalcini preferred grand gestures and big risks. As a child, she vowed never to marry, in order to devote herself completely to science—a promise she kept. Finishing school? No thanks. She was meant for medical school. When the Italian government barred her from medicine and research in 1938 because she was Jewish, she set up a secret lab in a bedroom so she could continue to examine the development of the cells of the nervous system, an interest she had cultivated while working toward her medical degree.

During this time, Levi-Montalcini read an article written by the founder of developmental neurobiology, a German scientist based in St. Louis, Missouri, named Viktor Hamburger. Hamburger used chick embryos—chicken offspring before they've hatched—to look into a possible link between the spinal cord and the development of the nervous system. The nervous system quickly transmits messages throughout the body through special cells called nerve cells. The idea of researching the spinal cord in relation to the nervous system piqued her interest. Even while operating undercover, Levi-Montalcini figured she could talk her way into a regular supply of chicken eggs.

She sprang into action, conducting her own experiments to see if she could discover a link. She recruited a former professor (also Jewish and barred from working) as a research partner and called on her family to provide lab support. Her brother built an incubator for the eggs she gathered, and Levi-Montalcini made a scalpel from a filed-down knitting needle. She also acquired a slew of tiny instruments, like forceps made for a watchmaker and scissors made for an ophthalmologist. She used these miniature tools to extract the chick embryos and cut their spines into thin slices. After studying the neurons (the cells of the nervous system) in the spinal cord at different stages of the chick's development before hatching, Levi-Montalcini discovered something entirely new: as a normal part of the chick's early development, nerve cells grew and nerve cells died.

Because she wasn't allowed to publish her research in Italy, Levi-Montalcini sent her papers to Swiss and Belgian journals available in America, which is where Hamburger learned about her work. After World War II concluded and Levi-Montalcini was allowed to conduct scientific experiments outside the bedroom, Hamburger invited her to Washington University in St. Louis to discuss their overlapping interests. She accepted, and a trip that should have taken a few months turned into a twenty-six-year tenure at the institution.

With their backgrounds and interests, Levi-Montalcini and Hamburger were an ideal match to tackle the mystery of how nerve cells emerge and extinguish. Levi-Montalcini thrived in her new environment, working extraordinarily hard from morning until late into the evening.

Levi-Montalcini believed that her biggest accomplishments were guided by intuition. "I have no particular intelligence," she said. But when the powerful weather vane inside her caught a direction or a thought, "I know it's true. It is a particular gift, in the subconscious. It's not rational."

Hamburger leaned toward crediting talent. "She has a fantastic eye for those things in microscope sections . . . and she's an extremely ingenious woman."

During a trip to Brazil to further her research (with mice in tow), Levi-Montalcini observed something extraordinary. She plopped some embryonic chick cells on one side of a petri dish and a chunk of tumor on the other. When placed next to each other—but not touching—the nerve fibers, astonishingly, started to stretch, extending from the cells in every direction like a fragile, otherworldly crown. It was an extraordinary show indeed—and one Levi-Montalcini took pleasure in playing over and over again throughout her career.

But this trick prompted an important question: what triggered the nerve fibers to grow? Upon her return to St. Louis, Levi-Montalcini figured it would take her a few months to find out.

A few months went by . . . and then a year, two, three; all the while, she and her then research partner, Stanley Cohen, continued to work furiously. (By that point, Hamburger had become more a mentor.) The team grew tumors, experimented with snake venom, and spent a lot of time thinking about mouse saliva. It took six years, until 1959, to identify what in a mouse's salivary gland made nerve cells grow. And then they had to purify it so that it would trigger that ethereal crown.

At one time, the discovery was seen as a small thing, impressive but also important only to a small area of science. But as more and more so-called growth factors were discovered, Levi-Montalcini's breakthrough became more important. We now know nerve growth factors influence everything from diseases that progressively damage our bodies to the success of a skin graft to protecting a damaged spinal cord.

In 1986, Levi-Montalcini and Cohen were awarded the Nobel Prize in Physiology for their work.

The prize made Levi-Montalcini an Italian celebrity. (She had returned to Italy part-time in 1961.) In her later years, she took work calls on the car phone as a driver chauffeured her around in a Lotus, a very fancy car. Levi-Montalcini was awarded the National Medal of Science, and in Italy she was appointed a senator for life. "The moment you stop working," she said, "you're dead." Wearing a string of pearls, high heels, and a brooch under her lab coat well into old age, Levi-Montalcini lived to be 103.

ROSALIND FRANKLIN

1920–1958
Genetics · British

"All her life, Rosalind knew exactly where she was going,"
Rosalind Franklin's mother recalled. Once her mind
latched on to something, she was all in. At age six, Franklin
was described by her aunt as "alarmingly clever. . . . She
spends all her time doing arithmetic for pleasure, [and] in-
variably gets her sums right." Franklin was precise, literal,
and always more at home with data than with speculation.

While Franklin was studying at Cambridge University,
her father complained that she felt about science as she
should about religion. Franklin held her ground. "You
frequently state . . . that I have developed a completely
one-sided outlook and look at everything and think of
everything in terms of science," she replied in a letter. "Ob-
viously my method of thought and reasoning is influenced
by a scientific training—if that were not so my scientific
training will have been a waste and a failure. . . . Science
and everyday life cannot and should not be separated."

When her father insisted she contribute to the World War II effort, science was a no-brainer. Following her graduation from Cambridge in 1941 and a research position, Franklin bicycled daily across an area of frequent air raids to a job she'd found at the British Coal Utilization Research Association. There her job was to figure out why some kinds of coal allowed gas and water to filter through it and why others put up a more efficient blockade. Charcoal had been used in gas masks, so it was important wartime research. Franklin published five papers on the material's properties by the time she was twenty-six. Her thesis, which covered "solid organic colloids with special reference to coal and related materials," earned her a PhD. Additionally, her research in the 1940s would help advance the eventual development of carbon fiber—a super-strong material we use in cars and airplanes.

After the war, a friend recommended her for a job in Paris as a physical chemist, again working on coal. The three years she spent abroad were perhaps her happiest. She made friends, spoke French flawlessly, and felt more at ease in her surroundings than she ever had at home. At age thirty, Franklin returned to England, drawn back by the feeling that London would accelerate her career.

Upon her return, she worked at King's College in London, where she took over the study of DNA. Although an interdisciplinary team had initiated the research, they had set it aside for the better part of a year. Franklin's goal was to figure out DNA's molecular structure. If someone made a model of the genetic information to be passed down from parents to children that could sit on the kitchen counter, what would it look like? To figure that out, Franklin lined up tiny DNA fibers, bundled them together, and x-rayed them to get an image.

At King's College, Franklin didn't have any formal collaborators. The most obvious choice would have been Maurice Wilkins, but an early misunderstanding about Franklin's role had turned the two colleagues into adversaries.

In 1952, a government committee asked Franklin to summarize her previous year's work. The scientist Max Perutz gave her summary to another group of researchers working on discovering the structure of DNA at Cambridge University: James Watson and Francis Crick. The paper was not marked confidential, but the report also wasn't intended for any eyes outside the committee. The report gave Watson and Crick crucial information about DNA. The pair also got hold of Franklin's X-ray photo of DNA without her knowing. Maurice Wilkins, the colleague she didn't get along with, showed the picture to Watson without Franklin's approval. Combined with Watson and Crick's own research, Franklin's information was enough for the Cambridge team to form a solid outline of DNA's structure. When they announced their discovery in the journal *Nature*—that DNA was a spiraled ladder, with one side going up and the other going down—they claimed the prize for finding the solution to DNA's structure without revealing Franklin's part in it.

Meanwhile, Franklin was on her way out at King's College. She felt that the environment wasn't good for her, and many of her colleagues agreed that she should leave.

As the discoverers were crowned, Franklin transferred to Birkbeck College. The transfer agreement between schools barred her from studying DNA.

At Birkbeck, Franklin set up a research group that looked at ribonucleic acid's role in virus reproduction. Her group was the best in the world, revealing, among other things, how proteins and nucleic acids fit together to transmit genetic information. To study polio—a disease that's transferred through contaminated food and water and causes paralysis—Franklin convinced a colleague's wife to sneak the virus on a plane to London by carrying it in a thermos.

Despite problems with Watson, Franklin became good friends with Crick and his wife, who was French. In Franklin's last year alive, her work got a moment of public recognition. For the 1958 Brussels World's Fair, she constructed a massive six-foot-tall display of the tobacco mosaic virus, a pathogen that affects hundreds of different plants.

Word of Franklin's essential part in the discovery of DNA did not get out until Watson himself spilled it. Since then, she's become the subject of several biographies and a poster child for those who don't receive the credit they deserve.

Today, the discussion of Franklin's life and work often rotates around one impossible question: Had she not died of ovarian cancer at the age of thirty-seven, would Franklin have shared the 1962 Nobel Prize with James Watson and Francis Crick? The answer is probably not.

The conclusion stings because there was some definite wrongdoing. In Watson's bestselling book *The Double*

Helix, which recounts his and Crick's discovery of DNA, Watson caricatured Franklin cruelly. She was "Rosy" (a name she did not like), who "might have been quite stunning had she taken even a mild interest in clothes." *Rosy,* who was curt and reactive and caused everyone working with her misery. *Rosy,* who could not possibly be considered serious competition in the quest to nail down the structure of DNA.

Because she had been dead for a decade when *The Double Helix* was published, others responded for her. It was "a mean, mean book," remembered the Nobel Prize–winning geneticist Barbara McClintock. Another geneticist, Robert L. Sinsheimer, called Watson's portrait of Franklin "unbelievably mean in spirit, filled with the distorted and cruel perceptions of childish insecurity." Anne Sayre, a friend and Franklin biographer, complained that Watson had "carelessly robbed Rosalind of her personality."

Watson's portrayal of Franklin, however, was made worse by this cavalier disclosure: Rosy "did not directly give us her data." And there it was, a stunning admission hidden between chapters of gloat. When others tugged on the dangling thread, the portrayal of Franklin began to unravel. Watson may have found her someone unpleasant to work with, but his experience was by no means universal. She was a competitor—and far ahead of Watson and Crick during much of the search for DNA. The rival pair simply wouldn't have made their discovery when they did had it not been for two crucial pieces of information passed from Franklin's lab at King's College in London to Watson and Crick's at Cambridge without her knowing it. Since *The*

Double Helix, many books and articles have been written about Franklin's very important role in the discovery of DNA.

Franklin, who was always deeply invested in data and facts, would have been happy to know that so many people cared about her concrete contributions.

ROSALYN SUSSMAN YALOW

1921–2011
Physics · American

If Rosalyn Yalow wanted to see Enrico Fermi speak, she would *see* Enrico Fermi speak—even if it meant hanging from the rafters. One of the world's greatest physicists talking about one of the world's greatest discoveries? She would be there even if she, a junior at Hunter College, had to compete for seat space with every physicist within traveling distance. Yalow did attend his colloquium at Columbia University. And she did see it while hanging from the rafters.

Such was the way with Rosalyn Yalow. Once an idea settled, the obstacles didn't stand a chance. How does a child get braces if her parents are poor? Yalow folded collars with her mother to bring in the necessary cash. How does a researcher secure lab space when she isn't given any? Yalow fashioned one of the first in the United States dedicated to radioisotope research out of a janitor's closet. How does one get past discrimination? "Personally," explained Yalow, "I have not been terribly bothered by it . . . if I wasn't going to do it one way, I'd manage to do it another way." That principle is how she navigated so many issues—graduate school rejections, work limits on pregnant women, rejection from a major journal, and, yes, a packed house for Enrico Fermi. She simply found another way—and quickly. Whining was a waste of time. Minutes were things she didn't like to lose.

Yalow was direct. She questioned colleagues at conferences and spoke up at meetings. At times, people found her manner abrasive, but Yalow sensed a double standard.

She and her longtime research partner, Solomon A. Berson, dealt in directness. Over the course of their twenty-two years working together, communication turned into what onlookers described as a sort of "eerie extrasensory perception." Their rapid-fire conversations about work would spill out into academic events, over dinners, and into walks around campus. At parties, Berson would have to remind Yalow to curb the shop talk and chat with other people.

They began working together at the Bronx Veterans Administration Hospital in 1950. Yalow had landed there three years earlier as a consultant via a full-time teaching position at Hunter College, and before that, a position at the Federal Telecommunications Laboratory. Yalow wanted to do nuclear physics, and neither Hunter nor the telecommunications lab was getting her any closer to that goal. Although it was in a closet at the VA hospital, she finally had her own lab. Berson was a resident physician, and Yalow brought him on board.

The pair clicked immediately. For eighty hours each week, they worked furiously on iodine metabolism, on the role of radioisotopes in blood volume determination, and on insulin research. With test tubes flying and chemical assays to prepare, there was never a moment to waste.

One of their first challenges as a team was to figure out how long insulin injected into a diabetic's body stays there. Insulin helps your body turn sugar into energy. A diabetic's body doesn't produce enough insulin, so the amount of sugar in the blood can get dangerously high. Injected insulin can help diabetics manage their condition. Yalow and Berson attached a radioactive tag to the insulin to monitor how long it stuck around. Through frequent blood sampling, they got their answer: too long.

Yalow and Berson traced the problem back to an incompatibility between the human body and the hormone injected, which in the 1950s came from pigs and cattle. (Today, insulin is synthetically made to exact human specifications to avoid this problem.)

The greatest takeaway from the experiment, however, was that they'd inadvertently developed a way to measure hormones—the secretions that help us regulate our body—in a test tube by looking at how our body responds to them. This process didn't require injecting radioactive material into the body and it was surprisingly accurate. They called their technique RIA, or radioimmunoassay.

Together, Yalow and Berson tore through hormone research, interpreting their discovery of RIA as a starting gun. What they learned enabled researchers to tell the difference between patients with type 1 and type 2 diabetes;

which children would benefit from human growth hormone treatments; whether ulcers should be operated on or
handled with medication; which newborns need medical
intervention for underactive thyroid . . . and the list goes
on. Though others were slow to catch on, within a decade, the RIA technique energized scientists, transforming
endocrinology—the study of hormones and other chemicals that regulate the way a body functions—into the "it"
specialty in medical research. For eighteen years, Yalow
and Berson knocked out hormone after hormone, furiously
preparing solutions and loading two to three thousand test
tubes in twenty-four-hour stretches.

By the time Berson moved on to City University of New
York in 1968, the pair had worked through much of RIA-
related research. Even so, Berson and Yalow reunited on
Tuesdays and Thursdays to pull all-nighters at the lab.

In a terrible one-two punch, Berson was hit with a small
stroke in March 1972 and then a heart attack during a scientific conference in Atlantic City one month later. The
heart attack killed him.

Berson and Yalow were so close that their relationship
was nearly familial, and his death hit Yalow extraordinarily hard. Besides losing her friend and research partner,
she was concerned about losing her status. For their entire partnership, his had been their outward-facing image.
Yalow was devastated by his death, but she also didn't
want the public's interest in her work to be buried with
Berson.

Yalow thought that going back to school for a PhD might
give her extra clout, but with so many years of important

research already under her belt, she decided against it. Making a name for herself—by herself—would require up-ending more than twenty years of assumptions that Berson led the partnership. (Yalow and Berson had always considered each other equals.)

The only way to regain the scientific community's trust, Yalow decided, would be to kick her already breakneck pace up a notch. She turned eighty-hour workweeks into hundred-hour ones. She renamed her lab the Solomon A. Berson Research Laboratory so that her articles—sixty produced in the following four years—would still appear with his name on them.

Yalow knew that her work with Berson deserved a Nobel, but science's highest award is given only to the living, and her partner was already gone. Yalow, as always, didn't give up hope. Every year, she chilled champagne and dressed up the day the awards were announced, just in case the news was good.

In the fall of 1977, Yalow woke up in the middle of the night, no longer able to sleep. As was her tradition, if sleep would not come, she'd go to the office. On this particular morning, she was in by 6:45. When she got word that she'd won the prize, Yalow ran home, changed her clothes, and was back in her lab by 8:00 a.m. Her Nobel was granted, but as an exception; both members of a research partnership should have been living.

The Nobel finally affirmed a desire she'd had since the age of eight: to become a "big deal" scientist. This time her admittance was granted with wide-open doors, not a spot in the rafters.

ACKNOWLEDGMENTS

Many of the extraordinary stories of discovery, creativity, and grit would not have been featured here were it not for scholars like Marilyn B. Ogilvie and writers like Sharon Bertsch McGrayne keeping them in the public discourse.

Beverly Horowitz believed that these extraordinary scientists should reach a wider audience, and her guidance and vision made it happen. Mackenzie Brady Watson is a tireless champion of these women and their stories. Her enthusiasm, encouragement, and ideas are a gift.

Domenica Alioto gave this girl and 52 others a chance. Rebecca Gudelis, Sarah Breivogel, Danielle Crabtree, and Claire Potter were amazing to work with—so sharp and incredibly lovely, all of them. Matt Wieland believed in this book from the beginning.

Stephen and Sharon Swaby were cheerleaders and expert advice-givers, in this and every other thing. Shirley Lindsay, Rosemary Christensen, and Marion Swaby are the trailblazing women whose stories I grew up with. Family members near and far were wonderfully supportive. Sean Swaby was an incredible hype man. Tim Leong was there for me at every point, from the center of the earth to the most distant star.

Gordon Lindsay, Elise Craig, Bryan Lufkin, Jordan

Crucchiola, Lydia Belander, Lexi Pandell, Julia Greenberg, Kevin Newcomen, and Brian Moyers offered invaluable feedback.

Susie Babcock, Jill Olsen, Kimberly Johnson, David Traversi, Joe Alves, Norm Ryan, Virginia Curtis, and Lisa Bonti were the teachers who inspired me to be a more creative and curious student and writer.

Thank you to the teachers and parents who asked for profiles about women in science, math, and technology geared for a younger audience. Their interest and initiative got this book going.

Thank you to Yvonne Brill for making a mean beef stroganoff . . . and for keeping communications satellites from slipping out of orbit. While discussion of the former helped get this book off the ground, here's hoping she'll be remembered for the latter.

NOTES

Introduction

"I would stand by the wall" Sofya Kovalevskaya, *A Russian Childhood,* trans. Beatrice Stillman, assisted by P. Y. Kochina. New York: Springer, 1978.

"As a research worker" Gerty Cori, *This I Believe,* hosted by Edward R. Murrow, September 2, 1952.

Technology and Invention

"The materials of science" Rachel Carson, *Lost Woods: The Discovered Writing of Rachel Carson,* edited by Linda Lear. Boston: Beacon Press, 1998.

Ada Lovelace

"the engine might compose" L. F. Menabrea, "Sketch of the Analytical Engine Invented by Charles Babbage, Esq.," trans. Augusta Ada Byron King, Countess of Lovelace, *Scientific Memoirs,* 1843.

"It can follow analysis" Ibid.

"the Analytical Engine weaves" Ibid.

"the most important paper" Allen G. Bromley, "Introduction." In H. P. Babbage, Volume 2: Babbage's Calculating Engines. Cambridge, MA: MIT Press, 1984. As cited in Ronald K. Smeltzer, Robert J. Ruben, and Paulette Rose, *Extraordinary Women in Science & Medicine: Four Centuries of Achievement.* New York: Grolier Club, 2013.

"[not] the first woman" Suw Charman-Anderson, "Ada Lovelace: Victorian Computing Visionary." Finding Ada. http://findingada.com/book/ada-lovelace-victorian-computing-visionary/, accessed August 29, 2014.

"I am much annoyed" As quoted in Dorothy Stein, *Ada: A Life and Legacy.* Cambridge, MA: MIT Press, 1985.

"all this was impossible" Ibid.

"That brain of mine" Ibid.

Hertha Ayrton

"astonished . . . one of their own sex" Evelyn Sharp, *Hertha Ayrton: 1854–1923, a Memoir.* London: E. Arnold & Company, 1926.

"Personally I do not agree" Ibid.

"for an original discovery" "Hughes Medal." The Royal Society, https://royalsociety.org/awards/hughes-medal/, accessed August 17, 2014.

"How can I answer" Hertha Ayrton, Census Form for *Census of England and Wales, 1911,* in *Extraordinary Women in Science & Medicine: Four Centuries of Achievement.* An Exhibition at the Grolier Club, September 18–November 23, 2013.

"An error that ascribes" Sharp, *Hertha Ayrton: 1854–1923, a Memoir.*

Hedy Lamarr

"[My father] made me" Gladys Hall, "The Life and Loves of Hedy Lamarr." Modern Romances, 1938. As cited in Rhodes, *Hedy's Folly: The Life and Breakthrough Inventions of Hedy Lamarr, the Most Beautiful Woman in the World.* New York: Vintage Books, 2012.

"Any girl can be glamorous" Richard Schickel, *The Stars.* New York: Dial, 1962.

"I've never been satisfied" Hall, "The Life and Loves of Hedy Lamarr." Modern Romances, 1938. As cited in Rhodes, *Hedy's Folly.*

"People who kid" As quoted in Rhodes, *Hedy's Folly.*

"It was a flop" Fleming Meeks, "I Guess They Just Take and Forget About a Person." *Forbes,* May 14, 1990. As cited in Rhodes, *Hedy's Folly.*

"Hedy Lamarr, screen actress" "Hedy Lamarr Inventor." *New York Times,* October 1, 1941.

"It's about time." As quoted in Rhodes, *Hedy's Folly.*

Ruth Benerito

"I'm not good with my hands" Agricultural Research Service, US Department of Agriculture, "Conversations from the Hall of Fame." http://www.ars .usda.gov/is/video/asx/benerito.broadband.asx, accessed August 31, 2014.

"Any number of people" Ibid.

"It was a good education" Ibid.

"I think that's what" Ibid.

"when [the government] put a lot of money" Ibid.

"I said I've been here" Ibid.

Stephanie Kwolek

"pulling a string" Paul W. Morgan and Stephanie L. Kwolek, "The Nylon Rope Trick: Demonstration of Condensation Polymerization." *Journal of Chemical Education,* April 1959.

"It wasn't exactly" Maureen Milford, "Mother of Invention Has Helped Save Thousands." *USA Today,* July 4, 2007.

"I never in a thousand" Ibid.

Grace Murray Hopper

"It's always easier to ask forgiveness" Diane Hamblen, Grace M. Hopper, and Elizabeth Dickason, "Biographies in Naval History: Rear Admiral Grace Murray Hopper, USN, 9 December 1906–1 January 1992." Naval History

and Heritage Command. http://www.history.navy.mil/bios/hopper_grace
.htm, accessed August 20, 2014.
"come back and haunt" Ibid.
"Where have you been" Uta C. Merzbach, "Computer Oral History Collection,
Grace Murray Hopper (1906–1992)." Computer Oral History Collection,
1969–1973, 1977, Archives Center, National Museum of American
History, July 1968.
"The instruction sequences" Ceruzzi, Paul, Introduction to *A Manual of
Operation for the Automatic Sequence Controlled Calculator.* Cambridge,
MA: MIT Press, 1946.
"We've always done it this way" Hamblen, Hopper, and Dickason,
"Biographies in Naval History," accessed August 20, 2014.
"They'll only be limited" Ibid.

Maria Mitchell

"One gets attached" Maria Mitchell, *Maria Mitchell: Life, Letters, and Journals.*
Boston: Lee & Shepard, 1896.
"sweeping the heavens" Ibid.
"For a few days" Ibid.
"It is really amusing" Ibid.
"I asked him" Ibid.
"It meant so much" Ibid.

Emmy Noether

"Frl. Noether is continually" As quoted in Sharon Bertsch McGrayne, *Nobel
Prize Women in Science: Their Lives, Struggles, and Momentous Discoveries.*
2nd ed. Washington, DC: National Academies Press, 2001.
"She won't be allowed to become a lecturer" Ibid.
"On receiving the new work" Ibid.
"an extraordinary professor" Ibid.
"You can make a strong case that her theorem" Natalie Angier, "The Mighty
Mathematician You've Never Heard Of." *New York Times,* March 26,
2012.
"Her heart knew no malice" McGrayne, *Nobel Prize Women in Science.*
"Fräulein Noether was the most significant" Albert Einstein, "The Late Emmy
Noether." *New York Times,* May 4, 1935.

Sophie Kowalevski

"I would stand by the wall" Sofya Kovalevskaya, *A Russian Childhood,* trans.
Beatrice Stillman, assisted by P. Y. Kochina. New York: Springer, 1978.
"learned women" Ibid.
"I was in a chronic state" Ibid.
"The meaning of these concepts" Ibid.
"Sofya immediately attracted" Ibid.

"The value" Ibid.
"brain of the deceased" Ibid.

Annie Jump Cannon

"Father was more interested" "Delaware Daughter Star Gazer." *Delmarva Star,*
 March 11, 1934.
"smoking like a small engine" Ibid.
"My success" Ibid.

Marguerite Perey

"In those days" "Madame Curie's Assistant: Scientific Battle Won, She's
 Losing Medical One." *Milwaukee Journal,* July 15, 1962.
"Under Marie Curie" Ibid.
"You are the second" Ibid.

Marie Tharp

"map-making in my blood" Marie Tharp, "Connect the Dots: Mapping the
 Seafloor and Discovering the Mid-Ocean Ridge." In *Lamont-Doherty Earth
 Observatory of Columbia: Twelve Perspectives on the First Fifty Years 1949–
 1999,* edited by Laurence Lippsett. Palisades, NY: Lamont-Doherty Earth
 Observatory of Columbia University, 1999.
"a once-in-the-history-of-the-world opportunity" Hali Felt, *Soundings: The Story of
 the Remarkable Woman Who Mapped the Ocean Floor.* New York: Henry
 Holt, 2012.
"great sea-gash" "Ocean Explorer: Soundings, Sea-Bottom, and Geophysics."
 National Oceanic and Atmospheric Administration. http://oceanexplorer
 .noaa.gov/history/quotes/soundings/soundings.html, accessed September
 10, 2014.
"a form of scientific heresy" Tharp, "Connect the Dots."
"girl talk" Ibid.
"No echo returned" Felt, *Soundings.*
"black cliffs in blue water" Ibid.
"Establishing the rift valley" Ibid.

Yvonne Brill

"I didn't really discuss it" Deborah Rice, "Interview with Yvonne Brill on
 November 3, 2005." Society of Women Engineers. http://www.djgcreate
 .com/swe/joomla/images/stories/brill/BRILLBRILL.pdf, accessed October
 26, 2013.
"There was just no question" Ibid.
"the cat's meow" Ibid.
"looking at the performance" Ibid.
"I never was afraid" Ibid.
"She truly represented" American Institute of Aeronautics and Astronautics,

"AIAA Mourns the Death of Honorary Fellow Yvonne C. Brill." https:
//www.aiaa.org/SecondaryTwoColumn.aspx?id = 16827, accessed
December 11, 2013.
"We believe in quality" Rice, "Interview with Yvonne Brill on November 3,
2005."

Sally Ride

"one thing I probably share" Cody Knipfer, "Sally Ride and Valentina
Tereshkova: Changing the Course of Human Space Exploration." NASA.
http://www.nasa.gov/topics/history/features/ride_anniversary.html#
.VDwXddR4pfF, accessed August 30, 2014.
"Weightlessness is a great equalizer" "An Interview with Sally Ride." *Nova* PBS.
https://www.youtube.com/watch?v = yb6vw9AmiLs, accessed August 30,
2014.
"a girl physics major" Lynn Sherr, *Sally Ride: America's First Woman in Space.*
New York: Simon & Schuster, 2014.
"unconscious (I assume) bias" Ibid.
"directly addresses the problems" Sally Ride, *NASA: Leadership and America's
Future in Space,* August 1987.
"a better weather report" Sherr, *Sally Ride: America's First Woman in Space.*

Ellen Swallow Richards

"that her admission did not" Records of the Meetings of the MIT Corporation,
December 14, 1870, *Archival Collection AC.*
"Had I realized" Caroline Louisa Hunt, *The Life of Ellen H. Richards.* Boston:
Whitcomb & Barrows, 1912.
"I have felt the greatest" First Annual Report to the Women's Educational
Association circa 1877, folder 9, Collection on the Massachusetts
Institute of Technology Women's Laboratory, 1867–1922 (AC 0298),
Institute Archives and Special Collections, MIT Libraries, Cambridge,
Massachusetts.

Anna Wessels Williams

"near-epidemic levels" John Emrich, "Anna Wessels Williams, M.D.: Infectious
Disease Pioneer and Public Health Advocate." *AAI Newsletter,* March/
April 2012.
"happy to have the honor" "Dr. Anna Wessels Williams," *Changing the
Face of Medicine.* National Library of Medicine, www.nlm.nih.gov
/changingthefaceofmedicine/physicians/biography_331.html, accessed
November 1, 2013.
"I was starting" The quote appeared in Regina Markell Morantz-Sanchez,
Sympathy & Science: Women Physicians in American Medicine. Chapel Hill:
University of North Carolina Press, 2000.
"to find out about" Ibid.

"a scientist of international repute" "94 Retired by City; 208 More Will Go."
    New York Times, March 24, 1934.

Alice Hamilton

"fourth-rate bacteriologist" Alice Hamilton, *Exploring the Dangerous Trades.*
    Boston: Little, Brown, 1943.
"as if I was going up in a flying machine" Ibid.
"As I prowled about the streets" Ibid.
"For years" Ibid.
"poisonous occupations" Ibid.
"tin foil" Ibid.
"leaded" Ibid.
"I was about the only" Ibid.
"No young doctor nowadays" Ibid.

Alice Ball

"The pit of Hell" Jack London, *The Cruise of the Snark.* New York: Macmillan,
    1911.

Helen Taussig

"the crossword puzzle" As quoted in Jody Bart, *Women Succeeding in the
    Sciences: Theories and Practices Across Disciplines.* West Lafayette, IN:
    Purdue Research Foundation, 2000.
"Who is going to be such a fool" Ibid.
"I close ductuses" Ibid.
"I suppose nothing would ever give" Ibid.
"Dr. Gross [of Harvard]" Ibid.
"the knights of Taussig" Ibid.
"You have your sadnesses" Jeanne Hackley Stevenson, "Helen Brooke Taussig,
    1898: The 'Blue Baby' Doctor." *Notable Maryland Women.* Cambridge,
    MD: Tidewater, 1977.

Elsie Widdowson

"The modern loaf" Jane Elliott, "Elsie—Mother of the Modern Loaf." *BBC
    News,* March 25, 2007.
"Tender loving care" As quoted in Margaret Ashwell, "Elsie May Widdowson,
    C.H., 21 October 1906 – 14 June 2000." *Biographical Memoirs of Fellows of
    the Royal Society,* December 1, 2002.
"A slight accident" Ibid.

Virginia Apgar

"Nobody, but nobody" "The Virginia Apgar Papers: Biographical Information."
    US National Library of Medicine. http://profiles.nlm.nih.gov/ps/retrieve
    /Narrative/CP/p-nid/178, accessed June 13, 2014.

"never sat down" Ibid.

"Frankly, how does she do it" Ibid.

"That's easy" "The Virginia Apgar Papers: Obstetric Anesthesia and a Scorecard for Newborns, 1949–1958." US National Library of Medicine. http://profiles.nlm.nih.gov/ps/retrieve/Narrative/CP/p-nid/178, accessed June 13, 2014.

"people doctor" "The Virginia Apgar Papers: The National Foundation–March of Dimes, 1959–1974." US National Library of Medicine. http://profiles .nlm.nih.gov/ps/retrieve/Narrative/CP/p-nid/178, accessed June 13, 2014.

"Her warmth and interest" Joseph F. Nee, memorial service, "The Virginia Apgar Papers." US National Library of Medicine. New York, September 15, 1974.

Jane Wright

"the mother of chemotherapy" Ronald Piana, "Jane Cooke Wright, MD, ASCO Cofounder, Dies at 93." *ASCO Post,* March 15, 2013.

"renowned artist" "Homecoming for Jane Wright." *Ebony,* May 1968.

"His being so good" As quoted in Lisa Yount, *Black Scientists.* New York: Facts on File, 1991.

"the Cinderella" Jane C. Wright, "Cancer Chemotherapy: Past, Present, and Future—Part I." *JAMA,* August 1984.

"It is almost, not quite, but almost" Ibid.

"Lollygagging" Alison Jones, personal interview, September 14, 2014.

"She was one of the few people" Ibid.

Florence Nightingale

"the symptoms or the sufferings" Florence Nightingale, *Collected Works of Florence Nightingale.* Waterloo, Ontario, Canada: Wilfrid Laurier University Press, 2009.

Jeanne Villepreux-Power

"power cages" Jeannette Power, "Observations on the Habits of Various Marine Animals." In *Annals and Magazine of Natural History.* London: Taylor and Francis, 1857.

"one of the most eminent" Matilda Joslyn Gage, "Woman as an Inventor." In *The North American Review,* edited by Allen Thorndike Rice. New York: AMS Press, 1883.

Mary Anning

"lively and intelligent" Charles Dickens, "Mary Anning, The Fossil Finder." *All The Year Round: A Weekly Journal,* July 22, 1865.

"I beg your pardon" Ibid.

"The carpenter's daughter" Ibid.

Barbara McClintock

"I didn't belong to that family" As quoted in Sharon Bertsch McGrayne, *Nobel Prize Women in Science: Their Lives, Struggles, and Momentous Discoveries.* 2nd ed. Washington, DC: National Academies Press, 2001.

"I had it done within two" As quoted in Evelyn Fox Keller, *A Feeling for the Organism: The Life and Work of Barbara McClintock.* New York: Henry Holt, 1983.

"it was so . . . obvious" Ibid.

"lapping up the stimulation she provided" As quoted in McGrayne, *Nobel Prize Women in Science.*

"very powerful work" Ibid.

"You're not conscious of anything else" As quoted in Keller, *A Feeling for the Organism.*

"like a lead balloon" As quoted in McGrayne, *Nobel Prize Women in Science.*

"I was startled" Ibid.

"All the surprises" Press conference on 1983 Nobel Prize, Ibid.

"discovery of mobile genetic elements" "The Nobel Prize in Physiology or Medicine 1983." Nobel Prize, http://www.nobelprize.org/nobel_prizes /medicine/laureates/1983/, accessed August 4, 2014.

Rachel Carson

"I had given up writing forever" Rachel Carson. *Lost Woods: The Discovered Writing of Rachel Carson,* edited by Linda Lear. Boston: Beacon Press, 1998.

"Every living thing of the ocean" Ibid.

"We live in a scientific age" Ibid.

"Almost immediately DDT was hailed" Rachel Carson, *Silent Spring.* New York: Houghton Mifflin, 1962.

"efforts which will prevent" "The National Environmental Policy Act of 1969," 42 U.S.C., January 1, 1970.

"the most important piece" Jack Lewis, "The Birth of EPA." *EPA Journal,* November 1985.

Ruth Patrick

"collected everything" Sandy Bauers, "Ruth Patrick: 'Den Mother of Ecology.'" *Philadelphia Inquirer,* March 5, 2007.

"a little peon" Ibid.

"You can't have society without industry" Michael Roddy, "Pollution Fears Come to Lakes, Springs," Associated Press, January 8, 1984.

"Come here at once" "Almost Had a War on Her Hands." *Sydney Morning Herald,* August 11, 1960.

"So you're the lady" Ibid.

"You see, diatoms are like detectives" Bauers, "Ruth Patrick: 'Den Mother of Ecology.'"

"I try not to think about it" Bauers, "Ruth Patrick: 'Den Mother of Ecology.'"

Rita Levi-Montalcini

"I have no particular intelligence" As quoted in Sharon Bertsch McGrayne, *Nobel Prize Women in Science: Their Lives, Struggles, and Momentous Discoveries.* 2nd ed. Washington, DC: National Academies Press, 2001.
"The moment you stop" Ibid.

Rosalind Franklin

"alarmingly clever" As quoted in Brenda Maddox, *Rosalind Franklin: The Dark Lady of DNA.* New York: HarperCollins, 2002.
"You frequently state" Ibid.
"might have been" James Watson, *The Double Helix: A Personal Account of the Discovery of the Structure of DNA.* New York: Scribner, 1968.
"a mean, mean book" As quoted in McGrayne, *Nobel Prize Women in Science.*
"unbelievably mean in spirit" Ibid.

Rosalyn Sussman Yalow

"Personally, I have not been terribly bothered by it" Sharon Bertsch McGrayne, *Nobel Prize Women in Science: Their Lives, Struggles, and Momentous Discoveries.* 2nd ed. Washington, DC: National Academies Press, 2001.
"eerie extrasensory perception" Ibid.
"big deal" Ibid.

BIBLIOGRAPHY

Ada Lovelace

"Charles Babbage: Pioneer of the Digital Age: An Exhibition at the Beinecke Library." Yale University Beinecke Rare Books & Manuscript Library. http://beinecke.library.yale.edu/exhibitions/charles-babbage-pioneer -digital-age-exhibition-beinecke-library, accessed September 15, 2014.

Charman-Anderson, Suw. "Ada Lovelace: Victorian Computing Visionary." *Finding Ada.* http://findingada.com/book/ada-lovelace-victorian-computing-visionary/, accessed August 29, 2014.

Menabrea, L. F. "Sketch of the Analytical Engine Invented by Charles Babbage, Esq.," trans. Augusta Ada Byron King, Countess of Lovelace, *Scientific Memoirs,* 1843.

Morais, Betsy. "Ada Lovelace: The First Tech Visionary." *The New Yorker,* October 15, 2013. http://www.newyorker.com/tech/elements/ada -lovelace-the-first-tech-visionary, accessed August 28, 2014.

Smeltzer, Ronald K., Robert J. Ruben, and Paulette Rose. *Extraordinary Women in Science & Medicine: Four Centuries of Achievement.* New York: Grolier Club, 2013.

Stein, Dorothy. *Ada: A Life and a Legacy.* Cambridge, MA: MIT Press, 1985.

Hertha Ayrton

Ayrton, Hertha. Census Form for *Census of England and Wales, 1911,* in *Extraordinary Women in Science & Medicine: Four Centuries of Achievement.* An Exhibition at the Grolier Club, September 18–November 23, 2013.

Byers, Nina, and Gary Williams. *Out of the Shadows: Contributions of Twentieth-Century Women to Physics.* New York: Cambridge University Press, 2006.

Grinstein, Louise S., Rose K. Rose, and Miriam H. Rafailovich, eds. *Women in Chemistry and Physics.* Westport, CT: Greenwood Press, 1993.

"Hughes Medal." The Royal Society. https://royalsociety.org/awards/hughes -medal/, accessed August 17, 2014.

Ogilvie, Marilyn Bailey. *Women in Science: Antiquity Through the Nineteenth Century.* Cambridge, MA: MIT Press, 1993.

Sharp, Evelyn. *Hertha Ayrton: 1854–1923, a Memoir.* London: E. Arnold & Company, 1926.

Smeltzer, Ronald K., Robert J. Ruben, and Paulette Rose. *Extraordinary Women in Science & Medicine: Four Centuries of Achievement.* New York: Grolier Club, 2013.

Hedy Lamarr

George, Antheil, and Markey Hedy Kiesler, assignee. Secret Communication System, Patent 2292387 A. August 11, 1942.

"Hedy Lamarr Inventor." *New York Times,* October 1, 1941.

Rhodes, Richard. *Hedy's Folly: The Life and Breakthrough Inventions of Hedy Lamarr, the Most Beautiful Woman in the World.* New York: Vintage Books, 2012.

Ruth Benerito

Agricultural Research Service, US Department of Agriculture, "Conversations from the Hall of Fame." http://www.ars.usda.gov/is/video/asx/benerito.broadband.asx, accessed August 31, 2014.

Condon, Brian D., and J. Vincent Edwards. "Cross-Linking Cotton." *Agricultural Research,* February 2009.

Fox, Margalit. "Ruth Benerito, Who Made Cotton Cloth Behave, Dies at 97." *New York Times,* October 7, 2013.

"Ruth Benerito." Lemelson-MIT Program, Massachusetts Institute of Technology, Cambridge, MA, August 31, 2014. http://lemelson.mit.edu/winners/ruth-benerito.

Wolf, Lauren K. "Wrinkle-Free Cotton." *Chemical & Engineering News,* American Chemical Society, December 2, 2013.

Yafa, Stephen. *Cotton: The Biography of a Revolutionary Fiber.* New York: Penguin Group, 2005.

Stephanie Kwolek

Lemelson Foundation. "1999 Lemelson-MIT Lifetime Achievement Award Winner Stephanie L. Kwolek." http://youtube/8dX3Z5CyF3c, accessed February 28, 2009.

Milford, Maureen. "Mother of Invention Has Helped Save Thousands." *USA Today,* July 4, 2007.

Morgan, Paul W., and Stephanie L. Kwolek. "The Nylon Rope Trick: Demonstration of Condensation Polymerization." *Journal of Chemical Education,* April 1959.

Norton, Tucker, personal interview, February 16, 2011.

Pearce, Jeremy. "Stephanie L. Kwolek, Inventor of Kevlar, Is Dead at 90." *New York Times,* June 20, 2014.

"Stephanie L. Kwolek." Chemical Heritage Foundation. http://www.chemheritage.org/discover/online-resources/chemistry-in-history/themes/petrochemistry-and-synthetic-polymers/synthetic-polymers/kwolek.aspx, accessed August 27, 2014.

Grace Murray Hopper

Ceruzzi, Paul. Introduction to *A Manual of Operation for the Automatic Sequence Controlled Calculator.* Cambridge, MA: MIT Press, 1946.

Hamblen, Diane, Grace M. Hopper, and Elizabeth Dickason. "Biographies in Naval History: Rear Admiral Grace Murray Hopper, USN, 9 December 1906–1 January 1992." Naval History and Heritage Command. http://www.history.navy.mil/bios/hopper_grace.htm, accessed August 20, 2014.

Merzbach, Uta C. "Computer Oral History Collection, Grace Murray Hopper (1906–1992)." Computer Oral History Collection, 1969–1973, 1977, Archives Center, National Museum of American History, July 1968.

Smeltzer, Ronald K., Robert J. Ruben, and Paulette Rose. *Extraordinary Women in Science & Medicine: Four Centuries of Achievement.* New York: Grolier Club, 2013.

Maria Gaetana Agnesi

Alexanderson, Gerald L. "About the Cover: Maria Gaetana Agnesi— A Divided Life." *Bulletin of the American Mathematical Society,* January 2013.

Mazzotti, Massimo. *The World of Maria Gaetana Agnesi, Mathematician of God.* Baltimore, MD: Johns Hopkins University Press, 2007.

Ogilvie, Marilyn Bailey. *Women in Science: Antiquity Through the Nineteenth Century.* Cambridge, MA: MIT Press, 1993.

Smeltzer, Ronald K., Robert J. Ruben, and Paulette Rose. *Extraordinary Women in Science & Medicine: Four Centuries of Achievement.* New York: Grolier Club, 2013.

Stigler, Stephen M. *Statistics on the Table: The History of Statistical Concepts and Methods.* Cambridge, MA: Harvard University Press, 1999.

Maria Mitchell

Mitchell, Maria. *Maria Mitchell: Life, Letters, and Journals.* Boston: Lee & Shepard, 1896.

"This Month in Physics History, Maria Mitchell Discovers a Comet." *American Physical Society.* http://www.aps.org/publications/apsnews/200610/history.cfm, accessed November 7, 2013.

Vassar Historian. "Vassar Encyclopedia: Maria Mitchell." *The Vassar Encyclopedia.* http://vcencyclopedia.vassar.edu/faculty/original-faculty/maria-mitchell1.html, accessed November 7, 2013.

Emmy Noether

Angier, Natalie. "The Mighty Mathematician You've Never Heard Of." *New York Times,* March 26, 2012.

Byers, Nina, and Gary Williams. *Out of the Shadows: Contributions of Twentieth-Century Women to Physics.* New York: Cambridge University Press, 2006.

Einstein, Albert. "The Late Emmy Noether." *New York Times,* May 4, 1935.

McGrayne, Sharon Bertsch. *Nobel Prize Women in Science: Their Lives, Struggles, and Momentous Discoveries.* 2nd ed. Washington, DC: National Academies Press, 2001.

Smeltzer, Ronald K., Robert J. Ruben, and Paulette Rose. *Extraordinary Women in Science & Medicine: Four Centuries of Achievement.* New York: Grolier Club, 2013.

Sophie Kowalevski

Cooke, Roger. *The Mathematics of Sonya Kovalevskaya.* New York: Springer-Verlag, 1984.

Cooke, Roger L. "The Life of S. V. Kovalevskaya." In Vadim Kuznetsov [ed.], *The Kowalevski Property.* Providence, RI: American Mathematical Society, 2002.

Kovalevskaya, Sofya. *A Russian Childhood.* Translated by Beatrice Stillman, assisted by P. Y. Kochina. New York: Springer, 1978.

Ogilvie, Marilyn Bailey. *Women in Science: Antiquity Through the Nineteenth Century.* Cambridge, MA: MIT Press, 1993.

Smeltzer, Ronald K., Robert J. Ruben, and Paulette Rose. *Extraordinary Women in Science & Medicine: Four Centuries of Achievement.* New York: Grolier Club, 2013.

Annie Jump Cannon

Bok, Priscilla F. "Annie Jump Cannon, 1863–1941." *Publications of the Astronomical Society of the Pacific,* June 1941.

Bruck, H. A. "Obituary: Dr. Annie J. Cannon." *Observatory,* 1941.

"Delaware Daughter Star Gazer." *Delmarva Star,* March 11, 1934.

"Dr. Annie Cannon Called 'One of 12 Greatest Living Women.'" *Milwaukee Journal,* April 7, 1936.

Ogilvie, Marilyn Bailey. *Women in Science: Antiquity Through the Nineteenth Century.* Cambridge, MA: MIT Press, 1993.

Marguerite Perey

Byers, Nina, and Gary Williams. *Out of the Shadows: Contributions of Twentieth-Century Women to Physics.* New York: Cambridge University Press, 2006.

Haines, Catharine M. C. *International Women in Science: A Biographical Dictionary to 1950.* Santa Barbara, CA: ABC-CLIO, 2001.

"Madame Curie's Assistant: Scientific Battle Won, She's Losing Medical One." *Milwaukee Journal,* July 15, 1962.

Rayner-Canham, Marelene F., and Geoffrey Rayner-Canham. *Women in Chemistry: Their Changing Roles from Alchemical Times to the Mid-Twentieth Century.* Philadelphia: Chemical Heritage Foundation, 2001.

Marie Tharp

Felt, Hali. "Marie Tharp: Portrait of a Scientist." *General Bathymetric Chart of the Oceans.* http://www.gebco.net/about_us/gebco_science_day/documents/gebco_sixth_science_day_felt.pdf, accessed September 10, 2014.

———, *Soundings: The Story of the Remarkable Woman Who Mapped the Ocean Floor.* New York: Henry Holt, 2012.

Fox, Margalit. "Marie Tharp, Oceanographic Cartographer, Dies at 86." *New York Times,* August 26, 2006.

Hall, Stephen S. "The Contrary Map Maker." *New York Times,* December 31, 2006.

Levin, Tanya. "Oral History Transcript—Dr. Marie Tharp." *American Institute of Physics.* http://www.aip.org/history/ohilist/22896_4.html, accessed September 10, 2014.

"Ocean Explorer: Soundings, Sea-Bottom, and Geophysics." National Oceanic and Atmospheric Administration. http://oceanexplorer.noaa.gov/history/quotes/soundings/soundings.html, accessed September 10, 2014.

"Remembered: Marie Tharp, Pioneering Mapmaker of the Ocean Floor." Earth Institute at Columbia University. http://www.earth.columbia.edu/news/2006/story08-24-06.php, accessed September 10, 2014.

Tharp, Marie. "Connect the Dots: Mapping the Seafloor and Discovering the Mid-Ocean Ridge." In *Lamont-Doherty Earth Observatory of Columbia: Twelve Perspectives on the First Fifty Years 1949–1999,* edited by Laurence Lippsett. Palisades, NY: Lamont-Doherty Earth Observatory of Columbia University, 1999.

Yvonne Brill

Martin, Douglas. "Yvonne Brill, a Pioneering Rocket Scientist, Dies at 88." *New York Times,* March 30, 2013.

Rice, Deborah. "Interview with Yvonne Brill on November 3rd, 2005." Society of Women Engineers. http://www.djgcreate.com/swe/joomla/images/stories/brill/BRILLBRILL.pdf, accessed October 26, 2013.

Wayne, Tiffany K. *American Women of Science Since 1900.* Santa Barbara, CA: ABC-CLIO, 2011.

Sally Ride

"An Interview with Sally Ride." *Nova* PBS. https://www.youtube.com/watch?v=yb6vw9AmiLs, accessed August 30, 2014.

Grady, Denise. "American Woman Who Shattered Space Ceiling." *New York Times,* July 23, 2012.

Knipfer, Cody. "Sally Ride and Valentina Tereshkova: Changing the Course of Human Space Exploration." NASA. http://www.nasa.gov/topics/history/features/ride_anniversary.html#.VDwXddR4pfF, accessed August 30, 2014.

"Mission to Planet Earth." NASA. http://www.hq.nasa.gov/office/nsp/mtpe
.htm, accessed August 30, 2014.

Ride, Sally. *NASA: Leadership and America's Future in Space,* August 1987.

Sherr, Lynn. *Sally Ride: America's First Woman in Space.* New York: Simon &
Schuster, 2014.

Ellen Swallow Richards

Clarke, Robert. *Ellen Swallow: The Woman Who Founded Ecology.* Chicago:
Follett Publishing Company, 1973.

"Ellen Swallow Richards." MIT History. http://libraries.mit.edu/mithistory
/community/notable-persons/ellen-swallow-richards/, accessed August
30, 2014.

Hunt, Caroline Louisa. *The Life of Ellen H. Richards.* Boston: Whitcomb &
Barrows, 1912.

Ogilvie, Marilyn Bailey. *Women in Science: Antiquity Through the Nineteenth
Century.* Cambridge, MA: MIT Press, 1993.

Talbot, H. P. "Ellen Swallow Richards: Biography." *Technology Review,* 1911.

Anna Wessels Williams

Barry, John M. *The Great Influenza: The Story of the Deadliest Pandemic in
History.* New York: Penguin Books, 2005.

Emrich, John. "Anna Wessels Williams, M.D.: Infectious Disease Pioneer
and Public Health Advocate." *AAI Newsletter,* March/April 2012.

Morantz-Sanchez, Regina Markell. *Sympathy & Science: Women Physicians
in American Medicine.* Chapel Hill: University of North Carolina Press,
2000.

"94 Retired by City; 208 More Will Go." *New York Times,* March 24, 1934.

Ogilvie, Marilyn Bailey, and Joy Dorothy Harvey. *The Biographical Dictionary
of Women in Science: Pioneering Lives from Ancient Times to the Mid-
Twentieth Century.* New York: Routledge, 2000.

Yount, Lisa. *A to Z of Women in Science and Math.* New York: Facts on File,
2008.

Alice Hamilton

"Alice Hamilton." *Chemical Heritage Foundation.* http://www.chemheritage
.org/discover/online-resources/chemistry-in-history/themes/public-and
-environmental-health/public-health-and-safety/richards-e.aspx, accessed
May 19, 2014.

Hamilton, Alice. *Exploring the Dangerous Trades.* Boston: Little, Brown, 1943.

Alice Ball

Encyclopædia Britannica Online. s. v. "leprosy." http://www.britannica.com
/EBchecked/topic/336868/leprosy, accessed October 14, 2014.

London, Jack. *The Cruise of the Snark.* New York: Macmillan, 1911.

Wermager, Paul, and Carl Heltzel. "Alice A. Augusta Ball: Young Chemist Gave Hope to Millions." *ChemMatters,* February 2007.

Helen Taussig

Altman, Lawrence K. "Dr. Helen Taussig, 87, Dies; Led in Blue Baby Operation." *New York Times,* May 22, 1986.

Bart, Jody. *Women Succeeding in the Sciences: Theories and Practices Across Disciplines.* West Lafayette, IN: Purdue Research Foundation, 2000.

Smeltzer, Ronald K., Robert J. Ruben, and Paulette Rose. *Extraordinary Women in Science & Medicine: Four Centuries of Achievement.* New York: Grolier Club, 2013.

Stevenson, Jeanne Hackley. "Helen Brooke Taussig, 1898: The 'Blue Baby' Doctor." *Notable Maryland Women.* Cambridge, MD: Tidewater, 1977.

Elsie Widdowson

Ashwell, Margaret. "Elsie May Widdowson, C.H., 21 October 1906–14 June 2000." Biographical Memoirs of Fellows of the Royal Society, December 1, 2002.

——, "Obituary: Elsie Widdowson (1906–2000)." *Nature,* August 24, 2000.

"Dr. Elsie Widdowson." *MRC Human Nutrition Research,* Elsie Widdowson Laboratory. http://www.mrc-hnr.cam.ac.uk/about-us/history/dr-elsie-widdowson-ch-cbe-frs/, accessed September 24, 2014.

Elliott, Jane. "Elsie—Mother of the Modern Loaf." *BBC News,* March 25, 2007.

"Elsie Widdowson." *Economist,* June 29, 2000.

"Elsie Widdowson." *Telegraph,* June 22, 2000.

Weaver, L. T. "Autumn Books: McCance and Widdowson—A Scientific Partnership of 60 Years." *Archives of Disease in Childhood,* 1993.

Virginia Apgar

Apgar, Virginia. Letter to Allen O. Whipple. Mount Holyoke College, Archives and Special Collections, Virginia Apgar Papers, MS 0504, November 29, 1937.

Nee, Joseph F. "Eulogy—Memorial Service for Dr. Virginia Apgar." Mount Holyoke College. Archives and Special Collections. L. Stanley James Papers. MS 0782, Box 2, Folder 2: Correspondence about Apgar 1973–1975, September 15, 1974.

"The Virginia Apgar Papers: Biographical Information." U.S. National Library of Medicine. http://profiles.nlm.nih.gov/ps/retrieve/Narrative/CP/p-nid/178, accessed June 13, 2014.

"The Virginia Apgar Papers: Obstetric Anesthesia and a Scorecard for Newborns, 1949–1958." U.S. National Library of Medicine. http://profiles.nlm.nih.gov/ps/retrieve/Narrative/CP/p-nid/178, accessed June 13, 2014.

"The Virginia Apgar Papers: The National Foundation–March of Dimes,

1959–1974." US National Library of Medicine. http://profiles.nlm.nih
.gov/ps/retrieve/Narrative/CP/p-nid/178, accessed June 13, 2014.

Jane Wright

Chung, King-Thom. *Women Pioneers of Medical Research: Biographies of 25
Outstanding Scientists.* Jefferson, NC: McFarland, 2010.

"Homecoming for Jane Wright." *Ebony,* May 1968.

Jones, Alison, personal interview, September 14, 2014.

Piana, Ronald. "Jane Cooke Wright, MD, ASCO Cofounder, Dies at 93."
ASCO Post, March 15, 2013.

Swain, Sandra M. "A Passion for Solving the Puzzle of Cancer: Jane Cooke
Wright, M.D., 1919–2013." *Oncologist,* June 2013.

Warren, Wini. *Black Women Scientists in the United States.* Bloomington:
Indiana University Press, 1999.

Webber, Bruce. "Jane Wright, Oncology Pioneer, Dies at 93." *New York
Times,* March 2, 2013.

Wright, Jane C. "Cancer Chemotherapy: Past, Present, and Future—Part I."
JAMA, August 1984.

Yount, Lisa. *Black Scientists.* New York: Facts on File, 1991.

Florence Nightingale

Bostridge, Mark. *Florence Nightingale: The Making of an Icon.* New York:
Farrar, Straus & Giroux, 2008.

Nelson, Sioban, and Anne Marie Fafferty. *Notes on Nightingale.* Ithaca, NY:
ILR Press, 2010.

Nightingale, Florence. *Collected Works of Florence Nightingale.* Waterloo,
Ontario, Canada: Wilfrid Laurier University Press, 2009.

Smeltzer, Ronald K., Robert J. Ruben, and Paulette Rose. *Extraordinary
Women in Science & Medicine: Four Centuries of Achievement.* New York:
Grolier Club, 2013.

Maria Sibylla Merian

Haines, Catharine M. C. *International Women in Science: A Biographical
Dictionary to 1950.* Santa Barbara, CA: ABC-CLIO, 2001.

"Maria Sibylla Merian: 1647–1717." National Museum of Women in the
Arts. http://nmwa.org/explore/artist-profiles/maria-sibylla-merian,
accessed September 7, 2014.

Todd, Kim. *Chrysalis: Maria Sibylla Merian and the Secrets of Metamorphosis.*
Orlando, FL: Harcourt, 2007.

Jeanne Villepreux-Power

Brunner, Bernd. *The Ocean at Home: An Illustrated History of the Aquarium.*
London: Reakton Books, 2003.

Encyclopædia Britannica Online. s. v. "Jeanne Villepreux-Power." http:

//www.britannica.com/EBchecked/topic/1759584/Jeanne-Villepreux
-Power, accessed October 14, 2014.

Gage, Joslyn Matilda. "Woman as an Inventor." In *North American Review*, edited by Allen Thorndike Rice. New York: AMS Press, 1883.

Groeben, Christiane. "Tourists in Science: 19th Century Research Trips to the Mediterranean." *Proceedings of the California Academy of Sciences*, 2008.

Power, Jeannette. "Observations on the Habits of Various Marine Animals." *Annals and Magazine of Natural History*. London: Taylor & Francis, 1857.

Mary Anning

Dickens, Charles. "Mary Anning, the Fossil Finder." *All the Year Round*, July 22, 1865.

Emling, Shelley. *The Fossil Hunter: Dinosaurs, Evolution, and the Woman Whose Discoveries Changed the World*. New York: Palgrave Macmillan, 2009.

Ogilvie, Marilyn Bailey. *Women in Science: Antiquity Through the Nineteenth Century*. Cambridge, MA: MIT Press, 1993.

Barbara McClintock

Keller, Evelyn Fox. *A Feeling for the Organism: The Life and Work of Barbara McClintock*. New York: Henry Holt, 1983.

McGrayne, Sharon Bertsch. *Nobel Prize Women in Science: Their Lives, Struggles, and Momentous Discoveries*. 2nd ed. Washington, DC: National Academies Press, 2001.

Nobel Prize, http://www.nobelprize.org/nobel_prizes/medicine/laureates/1983/, accessed August 4, 2014.

Rachel Carson

Carson, Rachel. *Lost Woods: The Discovered Writing of Rachel Carson*. Edited by Linda Lear. Boston: Beacon Press, 1998.

——, *Silent Spring*. New York: Houghton Mifflin, 1962.

Lear, Linda. *Rachel Carson: Witness for Nature*. New York: Henry Holt, 1997.

Lewis, Jack. "The Birth of EPA." *EPA Journal*, November 1985.

Mahoney, Linda. "Rachel Carson (1907–1964)." National Women's History Museum. http://www.nwhm.org/education-resources/biography/-biographies/rachel-carson/, accessed June 13, 2014.

"Rachel Carson Dies of Cancer. 'Silent Spring' Author Was 56." *New York Times*, April 15, 1964. http://www.nytimes.com/learning/general/onthisday/bday/0527.html, accessed June 13, 2014.

Rothman, Joshua. "Rachel Carson's Natural Histories." *The New Yorker*, September 27, 2012. http://www.newyorker.com/books/page-turner/rachel-carsons-natural-histories, accessed June 13, 2014.

Sideris, Lisa H., and Kathleen Dean Moore, eds. *Rachel Carson: Legacy and Challenge*. Albany: State University of New York Press, 2008.

Ruth Patrick

"Almost Had a War on Her Hands." *Sydney Morning Herald,* August 11, 1960.

Bauers, Sandy. "Ruth Patrick: 'Den Mother of Ecology.'" *Philadelphia Inquirer,* March 5, 2007.

Belardo, Carolyn. "Pioneering Ecologist Dr. Ruth Patrick Dies." Academy of Natural Sciences of Drexel University, accessed September 1, 2014.

Dicke, William. "Ruth Patrick, a Pioneer in Science and Pollution Control Efforts, Is Dead at 105." *New York Times,* September 24, 2013. http://www.nytimes.com/2013/09/24/us/ruth-patrick-a-pioneer-in-pollution-control-dies-at-105.html?pagewanted=all&_r=0, accessed September 1, 2014.

"Dr. Ruth Patrick." WHYY. http://www.whyy.org/tv12/RuthPatrick.html, accessed September 1, 2014.

"Lecture 2: Biodiversity—Tom Lovejoy—Los Angeles." Reith Lectures, *BBC.* http://www.bbc.co.uk/radio4/reith2000/lecture2.shtml, accessed September 2, 2014.

Patrick, Ruth. "Some Diatoms of Great Salt Lake." *Bulletin of the Torrey Botanical Club,* March 1936.

Roddy, Michael. "Pollution Fears Come to Lakes, Springs." Associated Press, January 8, 1984.

Rita Levi-Montalcini

McGrayne, Sharon Bertsch. *Nobel Prize Women in Science: Their Lives, Struggles, and Momentous Discoveries.* 2nd ed. Washington, DC: National Academies Press, 2001.

Smeltzer, Ronald K., Robert J. Ruben, and Paulette Rose. *Extraordinary Women in Science & Medicine: Four Centuries of Achievement.* New York: Grolier Club, 2013.

Rosalind Franklin

Maddox, Brenda. *Rosalind Franklin: The Dark Lady of DNA.* New York: HarperCollins, 2002.

McGrayne, Sharon Bertsch. *Nobel Prize Women in Science: Their Lives, Struggles, and Momentous Discoveries.* 2nd ed. Washington, DC: National Academies Press, 2001.

Watson, James. *The Double Helix: A Personal Account of the Discovery of the Structure of DNA.* New York: Scribner, 1968.

Rosalyn Sussman Yalow

McGrayne, Sharon Bertsch. *Nobel Prize Women in Science: Their Lives, Struggles, and Momentous Discoveries.* 2nd ed. Washington, DC: National Academies Press, 2001.

Smeltzer, Ronald K., Robert J. Ruben, and Paulette Rose. *Extraordinary Women in Science & Medicine: Four Centuries of Achievement.* New York: Grolier Club, 2013.

INDEX

CREDITS

Grateful acknowledgment is made to the following:

March of Dimes Foundation: excerpt from Joseph F. Nee's memorial service speech for Virginia Apgar, September 15, 1974, from The Virginia Apgar Papers, U.S. National Library of Medicine, New York. All rights reserved. Reprinted by permission of the March of Dimes.

Philadelphia Inquirer: excerpt from *Ruth Patrick: "The Den Mother of Ecology"* by Sandy Bauers, March 5, 2007, copyright © 2015. All rights reserved. Reprinted by permission of the *Philadelphia Inquirer.*

The British Library Board: excerpt from *Ada: A Life and Legacy* by Dorothy Stein, MIT Press, 1985, MS 37182-37201. All rights reserved. Reprinted by permission of the British Library Board.

The Milwaukee Journal: excerpt from *Madame Curie's Assistant: Scientific Battle Won; She's Losing Medical One* by Marguerite Perey, July 15, 1962. All rights reserved. Reprinted by permission of the *Milwaukee Journal.*

The National Academies Press: excerpt from *Nobel Prize Women in Science: Their Lives, Struggles, and Momentous Discoveries* by Sharon Bertsch McGrayne, copyright © 2001 by the National Academies of Sciences. All rights reserved. Reprinted by permission of the National Academies Press.

ABOUT THE AUTHOR

Rachel Swaby is the author of *Headstrong: 52 Women Who Changed Science—and the World*. A freelance journalist, Swaby has written for *Runner's World, Wired, The Atlantic,* and other publications. She lives in Brooklyn.

Visit her at rachelswaby.com and follow @rachelswaby on Twitter.